THE
WARDROBE
OF CHRIST

Putting on the Character of Jesus

Carrie D. Rogers

WESTBOW
PRESS®
A DIVISION OF THOMAS NELSON
& ZONDERVAN

All Scripture quotations, unless otherwise indicated, are taken from the Holy Bible, New International Version®. NIV®. Copyright © 1973, 1978, 1984 by International Bible Society. Used by permission of Zondervan. All rights reserved.

Scripture quotations marked NASB are from the New American Standard Bible. © The Lockman Foundation, 1960, 1962, 1963, 1968, 1971, 1972, 1973, 1975, 1977. Used by permission.

Scripture quotations taken from THE AMPLIFIED BIBLE, Copyright © 1954, 1958, 1962, 1964, 1965, 1987 by The Lockman Foundation. All rights reserved. Used by permission.

Scripture quotations are taken from the Holy Bible, New Living Translation, copyright ©1996, 2004, 2007 by Tyndale House Foundation. Used by permission of Tyndale House Publishers, Inc., Carol Stream, Illinois 60188. All rights reserved.

Scripture taken from The Message. Copyright © 1993, 1994, 1995, 1996, 2000, 2001, 2002. Used by permission of NavPress Publishing Group.

WestBow Press books may be ordered through booksellers or by contacting:

WestBow Press
A Division of Thomas Nelson & Zondervan
1663 Liberty Drive
Bloomington, IN 47403
www.westbowpress.com
1 (866) 928-1240

Because of the dynamic nature of the Internet, any web addresses or links contained in this book may have changed since publication and may no longer be valid. The views expressed in this work are solely those of the author and do not necessarily reflect the views of the publisher, and the publisher hereby disclaims any responsibility for them.

Any people depicted in stock imagery provided by Thinkstock are models, and such images are being used for illustrative purposes only. Certain stock imagery © Thinkstock.

ISBN: 978-1-4908-9807-0 (sc)
ISBN: 978-1-4908-9808-7 (e)

Print information available on the last page.

WestBow Press rev. date: 10/19/2015

To Erik:
who loves me more

CONTENTS

INTRODUCTION

**Therefore, as God's chosen people, holy and dearly loved, clothe yourselves
with compassion, kindness, humility, gentleness and patience. Bear
with each other and forgive one another if any of you has a grievance
against someone. Forgive as the Lord forgave you. And over all these
virtues put on love, which binds them all together in perfect unity.
Colossians 3:12-14**

Welcome to *The Wardrobe of Christ*. I'm thrilled that you have decided to embark on this journey with me. This book in your hands is my first attempt at a written Bible study. The months I have spent with God preparing this study have changed me forever. I knew putting a study on paper would be a challenge, but I had no idea of the adventure before me.

I want you to know before you begin that I am not writing this study out of my knowledge and experience on the matter. I am not a Biblical scholar. Like you, I am (at best) a pursuer of Jesus. Plain and simple – I want to know Him more. In my pursuits, God has provided me with the opportunity to put on paper what He is teaching me.

Each of the six chapters is broken up into five daily lessons. If you look at the Table of Contents, you will notice that the first two chapters look different than the last four. The content in chapters one and two serve as a foundation for the rest of the study. Please note: "foundational" does not mean basic or boring. There are teachable moments starting in Chapter one, day one, so come expecting! A Leader Guide is provided at the back of the study with questions to help facilitate group discussion.

I'm primarily studying out of the *New International Version* of the Bible. Feel free to use whichever God-inspired translation you prefer; however, if you do have an NIV translation, you may want to use it. In the places where I ask you to fill in the blank, the answers will be found directly from the pages of a NIV Bible. There are many websites that offer different translations that you can use as well. A few of my favorites are: www.biblegateway.com, www.blueletterbible.org and www.bible.org. Also, unless otherwise noted, I'm using bible.org as my source for Hebrew and Greek definitions.

Most importantly I want you to know that I am praying for you. I'm praying that you'll approach this study with your heart wide open to what God wants teach you - that you'll experience the Lord in a fresh and exciting way - that God will grow in you a desire for more of Him. Lastly, I'm praying that we all learn to put on the wardrobe of Jesus Christ.

CHAPTER 1

CLOTHED IN CHRIST

Getting dressed each day is important. But it's also a daily chore - this putting on of clothes. Wouldn't you agree? Some days I do the clothing thing well. I put thought into my wardrobe and walk out the door looking put together. Other days I get by. Barely. The poor innocent bystanders at my daughter's preschool are the most unfortunate victims of my early morning dressing routine. Each and every morning they see me at drop-off in the same comfy pants and T-shirt, my hair pulled back with no makeup on. Trust me, it isn't a pretty sight.

One day, during this daily chore of dressing, the quiet voice of the Lord began talking to me about the importance of what I put on each day. Although I would have loved some "what should I wear today" advice as I stared blankly at the clothes in my closet, I realized that God wasn't talking to me about what I needed to put on physically. His focus, not surprising, was geared toward the spiritual. The next few weeks, He began leading me to many familiar verses from His Word that deal with the issue of "putting on"... And so my studying began.

Throughout this study we'll be inspecting the wardrobe of none other than Jesus Christ. But we won't be focusing on what's lining the walls of His heavenly closet. Instead, we're going to be studying the attributes that adorn the Son of God.

DAY 1
EVERYDAY JESUS

Read Romans 13:14. Write the verse in the space provided.

I really like the sound of that – to be clothed with the Lord Jesus Christ. There is nothing in my closet and nothing in any retail store that would be of greater worth. The word "clothed" in the Greek is *enduo*, which means "to sink into, put on, clothe one's self."

What kind of clothes do you like to sink into?

When I am sinking into something, I guarantee it's going to be something comfortable. I've never *sunk in* to a tailored dress or a pair of stilettos. Pajama pants and a T-shirt is my usual go-to. When I'm dressed up, the first thing I do when I get home is sink into something more comfortable.

That's what I love about this verse. When we clothe ourselves with Jesus, we're not putting on something stuffy and formal. We're putting on the very thing that we love the most, the thing that makes us the most comfortable, the thing that makes us feel the most at home.

Do you think about Jesus that way? Is Jesus "comfort wear" to you?

❑ **Yes**
❑ **No**

Why or why not?

For those of you who have a hard time picturing Jesus as someone you want to be comfortable with, let me ask you this: do you remember when you learned to ride a bike for the first time?

A couple of years ago I experienced the adventure of life on a bicycle through the eyes of my eldest daughter, Haley. She was so excited to get a new, bigger bike. She had her eyes set on a pink one with a basket attached to the front – just the right size for her purse or any other necessity she might need on the road. Of course this perfect bike had no training wheels. As we wheeled her new bicycle down the driveway, I could see the thrill in my precious one's eyes. That is until she sat her tiny rump on the seat and tried to push off the curb for the first time. Fear flashed across her face as she quickly lost balance and fell. Suddenly, her beautiful new bike was just not comfortable.

It took a little convincing, but eventually Haley did learn to stay on that fancy pink bike. With a little practice and loads of faith in her mommy's tight grip on the back of her seat, she learned to ride with comfort and ease.

I'm not saying that life with Jesus is like riding a bike. However, maybe understanding how comfort can change with time, as it does with learning to ride a bike, will help you to imagine a time when your comfort with our God might change too.

The amazing truth is if you are in a personal relationship with Jesus you have already made the first step in being clothed with Him.

Read Galatians 3:26-27. Note when the Lord became part of your wardrobe.

On the day of your salvation, Jesus provided the spiritual clothing needed for each day. Now it's our job to choose to put on His likeness each and every day. God will not force Himself upon us, but He is delighted each day when we choose to fully step into our relationship with Him.

Essentially, Jesus wants to become our "everyday wear".

Read John 15:4. Fill in the blanks below.

"_____ in me and I will _____ in you."

Most translations read "remain" but I love the seldom-used word in the King James Version: abide. The word *abide* means, "to remain, to continue to be present, to be held, to endure, to remain as one."[1] Read this definition again and underline the words that stand out most to you.

It's no wonder this word *abide* is so scarcely heard. What a rare thing it is to continually stay connected to anybody. We live in a world where every commitment can easily be broken. There's always a way out, a loophole or a backdoor to take if something better comes along. You don't have to look far to see the covenant of marriage unraveling. Ask almost anyone in the business world; they'll tell you our word is no longer our bond.

With one word, abide, we are invited to participate in a sacred never-ending romance with our Savior. "Abide in me and I will abide in you." Jesus is asking us to commit ourselves and remain connected to Him for the long haul.

Read Matthew 11:28-30.

A yoke is a wooden bar or frame by which two animals (like oxen) are joined together at the head or neck for working together. This illustration gives Jesus' listeners a picture of what it looks like to abide in Him. The yoke is a picture of being physically connected to Jesus.

In Matthew 11:28 when Jesus bids us to come, He is actually inviting us to come and stay. He never intended for you and me to come and go depending on when we think we need Him, although that's how most of us function in our everyday walk. Jesus' initial intention – His true intention – is "come and stay." Jesus desires unbroken fellowship with us, where our whole lives might be spent in complete intimacy with Him.

Consider this: "Who would, after seeking the King's palace, be content to stand in the door, when he is invited in to dwell in the King's presence, and share with Him in all the glory of His royal life? Oh, let us enter in and abide, and enjoy to the full all the rich supply His wondrous love hath prepared for us!"[2]

> **When you think about your relationship with Jesus, do you think you have spent more time in the doorway or have you enjoyed the blessing of living in the presence of the King of Kings? Why?**

We have done well to come, but we would be doing much better if we were to come and stay. Like your favorite pair of well-worn jeans, put on Jesus when you get up in the morning. Make Him a part of your everyday wear. He's truly the only One worth the closet space.

DAY 2
DO YOU KNOW WHOM YOU'RE WEARING?

When we get dressed each day, we clothe ourselves intentionally. I have never walked by a mirror and thought, "Now how did that shirt get on me? Where did these shoes come from? Who put this outfit together?" Getting dressed doesn't happen by accident. Sometimes we carelessly forget to put something on (I have been known to leave the house without shoes), but what makes it onto the body was put there with intention.

I may go through the day completely unprepared because of what I forgot to *put on,* but you can be sure if it's on me, I put it there on purpose. The same is true when we get dressed each day spiritually.

> **Read Romans 13:14 again below. Put a box around the specific wording that Paul uses when naming "whom" we are to put on.**
>
> **"Rather clothe yourselves with the Lord Jesus Christ and do not think about how to gratify the desires of the sinful nature."**

Make no mistake – Paul was intentional in clumping these three powerful names of our Savior together. We must make certain, with the same level of purpose, that we are confident in whom we are putting on. He is the Lord Jesus Christ.

Let's look at each of these three titles.

LORD: HIS POSITION

The Greek word for *Lord* is *kurios,* which means, "the owner; one who has control of the person, the one who has might and power, master, to give authority, ruler of the universe." The equivalent word to *kurios* from the New Testament is the Hebrew word *Jehovah* in the Old Testament. Jehovah means "the existing One, the one true God, I am that I am." This name was held by the Jews to be so sacred that it was never pronounced out loud, except by the high priest when he entered into the most holy place. Whenever this name occurred in the sacred books, they pronounced it, as they still do, "Adonai" (Lord), thus using another word in its place.

To call Jesus Lord is no small task. When we choose to put Him on as Lord, we're giving Him permission to take His rightful position in our lives. We're choosing to submit ourselves to Him as the One with all authority to rule.

Read Romans 14:7-9. Fill in the blanks.

We _____ to the _____. (Verse 8)

What does it mean to you that you _belong_ to the Lord?

Have you ever struggled with the concept of truly giving the Lord authority in your life? Explain.

JESUS: HIS PURPOSE

Jesus was the given name of the Son of God. Father God divinely appointed it. The custom of naming a child in Biblical times carried great significance. It was the first and most important experience of a newborn Hebrew. Unlike today when children are given a first, middle and last name, each Hebrew child was given only one name at birth. This name was usually a reflection of the parent's wishes for the child or it was a prophet description of their personality.

Matthew explains the Christian significance of the name Jesus.

Read Matthew 1:21. Write down the reference to the name's meaning.

Jesus came to Earth with a specific purpose: to save. When we put Him on as Jesus, we're admitting that we're in need of a Savior. It is only through Jesus that we have abundant life.

Read Ephesians 2:8-9. According to verse 8, what are we saved by?

Jesus alone saves us. He is our gift of grace.

Think about a time when you experienced the gift of God's grace – a time when you received the unmerited favor of God when you know you absolutely didn't deserve it. Record your thoughts.

CHRIST: HIS PROMISE

The last name, Christ, is of essential importance because it makes an assertion about the human Jesus that differentiates Him from all other men. Christ is defined as, "the Messiah, the anointed One, consecrated for sacred duty, the King, the deliverer."

Desperate to be saved from oppression and political injustice, Israel has eagerly anticipated a messiah. Yet, sadly, counterfeit deliverers have plagued the Jews. There have been many false christs both in present day and in the past who have claimed to be the promised Messiah, but only Jesus Christ lived to perfectly fulfill all the Messianic prophecies of the Old Testament. No other man could prove to be the Anointed of God. Jesus is the only true Christ.

When we put Him on as Christ, we're saying that He is our promised deliverer (John 4:25-26). Jesus Christ is the Anointed of God who came in fulfillment of ancient prophesies. But more than that, He's the promise of the written Word. He's the promise of a relationship with the Father. He's the promise of eternal life. Wrapped up in Jesus Christ is the promise for life and godliness through the knowledge of Him who has called us by His own glory and goodness (2 Peter 1:3)

Read Matthew 16:13-20.

Jesus questioned His disciples, "Who do you say that I am?" He wanted to know if they were settled on the foundational issue of His identity.

By faith, who did Peter say He is?

Who did Jesus say had revealed this to Peter?

If Jesus came down from heaven today and asked you the same question, would you be able to answer as boldly as Peter?

Is He your Lord: the ONE in charge of your day to day?
Is He your Savior: the ONE who saves you from sin and self?
Is He your Messiah: your ONE hope of the promises of God for you?

Which of the three names of the Son of God resonate most with you? Why?

DAY 3
THE OTHER SIDE OF THE STORY

Begin today by reading Romans 13:14 given below.

"Rather clothe yourselves with the Lord Jesus Christ and do not think about how to gratify the desires of the sinful nature."

We have arrived at the point of conflict: The desire to clothe ourselves with Jesus versus continually thinking about how to satisfy our sinful nature. The word for sinful nature in Greek is *sarx,* and is defined as *"the flesh, the earthly nature apart from divine influence, and therefore prone to sin and opposed to God."*

There it is ladies, our flesh. Straight out of the womb, dressed in nothing but our birthday suits, we're born in opposition to God. However, things didn't start that way. Let's look back at a time when the flesh wasn't sinful and clothes didn't exist.

Read Genesis 2:22-25. Fill in the blanks below.

"The man and his wife were both _____, and they felt no _____."

God planted a garden, a literal paradise, and gave it to Adam. There Adam and Eve walked with God. They were naked and unashamed. What a beautiful picture of creation living in harmony with the Creator. Physically, emotionally and spiritually they lay bare before their God and each other. Sweet innocence. Perfect fellowship. Naked. But as we all know, this perfect paradise didn't last for long. Our sweet, unclothed Eve was deceived.

Read Genesis 3:6-7. What was the first thing Adam and Eve realized after they ate from the tree of the knowledge of good and evil?

Now that's a feeling I can relate to. Cover me, quick! I don't want to be seen naked! Sin. Loss of innocence. Shame. Guilt. It all hit them so quickly that all they could think to do was grab some fig leaves and cover up. After they had a little heart to heart with God, something had to be done about their new apparel. "The Lord God made garments of skin for Adam and his wife and clothed them." (Genesis 3:21)

What did God use for His creation's new apparel?

From the moment Eve's teeth touched the apple, a sacrifice was required. The hand of God shed the blood of an innocent animal, and clothes were fashioned from the animal's skin to be a covering for Adam and Eve. A big step up from a fig leaf. Thank you, God!

The first couple was no longer suited for the Garden of Eden. They were forced to leave comfort, security and most of all, perfect fellowship with the Father. As they walked out of paradise, they began walking in what we now know as the flesh. Sin had entered the world.

Romans 13:14 says, "… and do not think about how to gratify the desires of the sinful nature."

How do we gratify the desires of our sinful nature? According to translation, we are to "give no provision for the flesh." In this particular instance, the Greek word for "provision" is *pronoia,* which means, "forethought, providential care, to make provision for a thing." Excuse the analogy, but our flesh is a loaded gun. It's armed and ready for the sinful nature to have its way with us. Paul is commanding us to not think of pulling the trigger.

When my friend was on bed rest with her last pregnancy, she was given a medication that wouldn't allow her to eat grapefruit. So, guess which fruit she craved for the next 10 weeks? You got it: grapefruit. Apart from God, the flesh wants what it can't have. Period. The longing for that which is forbidden is the provision this verse is describing.

For generations after Adam and Eve, man walked in a way that was dominated by the flesh. They lived to gratify their sinful nature. Genesis 6:5 says that "The Lord saw how great man's wickedness on earth had become, and that every inclination of the thoughts of his heart was only evil all the time." Did you catch that? EVERY inclination of the thoughts of man's heart was ONLY evil ALL of the time. Man was dominated by his sinful nature and God grieved deeply. Because of the corruption on the Earth, God destroyed all of human life under the heavens, save one righteous man, Noah, and his family.

> **Can you think of a time in your life when you lived a life dominated by your flesh? Did you make a conscious decision to do life "your way" or were you ignorant of your sinful behavior?**

When the Ten Commandments were inscribed in stone, everything changed. The Law was spoken and boundaries were put into place. The flesh was now held to a new standard.

Read Romans 7:7-9.

Check the boxes that apply to Paul's teaching in the text.

❏ **The law is sin.**
❏ **The law makes me aware of sin.**
❏ **It's the Laws fault that I sin.**

Until our sinful nature met truth there was no measuring stick. Man didn't know that coveting was harmful until the law established it as such. However the law did more than give man boundaries. It also gave the sinful nature something to rebel against.

If you have children, you don't have to look far to see rebellion at work. When each of my children started crawling it was as though they were drawn to the things they couldn't and shouldn't touch. The wall outlets were like magnets to their chunky little fingers. As soon as their eyes locked in on the target, they were off – ready to stick whatever objects they could grab into the tiny little holes. It was my responsibility to protect them from danger by bringing in the Law. The socket was quickly established as a "no-no." Like perfect little angels, they happily crawled off to find something else to entertain them. WRONG! In an instant, the "no-no" became all the more interesting. Baby wants what baby can't have!

Can you give another example (using adults this time) of how the flesh rebels against the law of Truth?

We were all born with a sinful nature. As we have discussed, the flesh lives to rebel against the Law. Father God gave His people a set of rules they had no hope of following perfectly. What better way for Him to bring His people to awareness of their desperate need for a Savior.

DAY 4
LESSONS ON THE WAY OUT - PART 1

Today we are going to start by using our imaginations. Put yourself in the shoes of Adam and Eve and think about what they might have experienced on their journey from garden life to life in the world. Along the way, we'll stumble upon some important lessons about life outside the garden.

In the garden, every day was heaven on Earth: the perfect scenery and the perfect company. It was just the three of them: Adam, Eve and God. They probably walked together every day, laughing, talking and enjoying every intimate moment together. Adam and Eve experienced a life of total security, trusting God explicitly for every detail of their day. I'm sure they knew the exact lines of God's mouth as He smiled at them in sheer delight. They knew what it felt like to lean back against Him as they rested under the canopy of trees. They knew the sound of His voice and the sweet scent of His presence blowing through the breeze. But then – another voice, the deception, the apple, the bite. Everything changed.

As they walked away from the garden, imagine the separation they instantly felt. All of a sudden God seemed so far away – so distant – as if an invisible wall had been erected between them somehow.

What feelings do you think they felt as they kicked through the dirt towards their new home? (Could it be some of the feelings you and I have about God as we navigate through our own deserts?)

Is shame on your list somewhere? I have tried to create physical distance between God and myself out of shame and guilt. I've believed the voice in my head telling me that this time I'd really messed things up - that God's love for me had a limit and my time was now up.

Lesson #1: There's a battle for your thought life.

Read Romans 7:22-23.

Paul is describing the battle of our sinful nature and the tension that lies within. Do you realize that Satan, the Father of Lies, has waged war against the thoughts of our minds? His goal is to keep us from experiencing true life in Christ. His is plan of attack is through our thought life. He does this by giving us thoughts (based on a lie), usually using first person, singular pronouns (I, me, my).

Let me give an example based on our previous discussion. When I have wronged God, instead of trusting in His unmerited forgiveness, I might have this thought, "God will never forgive *me* for this. *I've* let him down again. *I'm* such a loser." Notice the use of pronouns. Satan plants thoughts like these in our heads, hoping to isolate us from truth and ultimately separate us from God.

Our feelings, then, respond to whatever our mind is set on. If you believe that you are a loser, you will begin to *feel* like a loser. You might start separating yourself from a crowd, confident that you won't fit it. You'll question why your friends like you or if you have any real friends.

Based on this example, are your feelings based on a truth or a lie?

Based on this example, can your feelings be trusted? Circle one: Yes or No

Contrary to what the world tells us, our feelings cannot be our measure of truth. Below are some scenarios that are played out in the lives of women today. Read each one and consider the danger of living according to our feelings.

1. You've budgeted $50 for clothing for the month. Your son really needs new shoes for school. You walk into a store and find an incredible sale in the women's department and everything seems to be in your size. You know that this money was set aside specifically for your son's shoes, but instead you spend the entire $50 on yourself. After all, you never do anything for yourself and you deserve it!

2. Your husband comes home from work and tells you that he had a horrible day. Nothing went right for him: he had to fire someone, he didn't make his bonus, and now he's going to have to travel for the next three months to make up for it. You know in your head that he has every right to be upset. You want to be a safe place for him – the one he can come to for comfort – but instead you let him have it. It's just so typical of him: Did he ask about your day? Of course not! The kids were out of control and getting on your last nerve, the house is a mess, and dinner is still not on the table. On top of that, all you can think about is doing it all *alone* for the next three months while he gets to travel all by himself.

3. At work, there is a man. He talks to you and says all the right things. He seems to genuinely care about you. He doesn't see all your faults, makes you feel like you're important, smart and fun to be around. But, he's married. You're not doing anything physically wrong with him, but you know in your head that your conversation with this man is not honoring to his wife. You don't care, though, because he makes you feel so good about yourself. How could that be so wrong?

Each one of these situations describes a woman whose thoughts have taken control. Remember, if we don't control our thought life, Satan will use our thoughts to control us. The Father of Lies loves to fill our minds with everything but the truth. Just as he did with Eve in the garden, his methods are sneaky and full of twisted half-truths.

How do we learn to discern the truth?

Read John 17:17. Fill in the blanks below.

"Your _____ is _____."

The only way to discern the truth is to know the Word of God. Although the world preaches, "Follow your heart and do what feels right," God sets a different standard. All of our thoughts (and feelings, for that matter) must be evaluated according to the standard of His Word. It's the only way to distinguish between truth and a lie.

Evaluate your thoughts and feelings today. Do they line up with the Truth of God's Word?

DAY 5
LESSONS ON THE WAY OUT - PART 2

Today we are going to continue to use our imaginations to picture life outside of the Garden. I understand that for some this exercise is difficult, but it's important to use our imaginations when approaching God's Word. These people we are reading about had real flesh and blood. The story of their lives played out just as authentically as our lives do today. When you read, don't be afraid to let your imagination take you beyond the black and white words on the page. Allow the Scriptures to come to life in your mind and trust God to give you a greater level of understanding as you read.

Lesson #2: Independence is NOT the goal.

Days and weeks may have passed since the dramatic exit from the Garden. I wonder if Adam and Eve decided that it was time to start living with some independence. Maybe it was time they start learning to do a few things on their own. Did they really need to rely on God for everything? Sure, God would be there when they needed Him, but they needed to start pulling some of their own weight out in the real world, right?

Have you ever felt that way? Have you ever thought to yourself, "How many times am I going to have to ask God for help? When am I going to learn to do this on my own?" Ladies – that's not garden talk. That is flesh talk! God's not interested in us figuring everything out on our own. He wants us to learn to live as they did in the garden – totally dependent on Him for everything.

Practically speaking, what does it mean to live a life of total dependence on God? What does that look like (or what could that look like) in your life?

Look up the following verses. List the benefits of trusting in your Heavenly Father with every ounce of your being.

Psalm 37:4-6

Proverbs 3:5-6

Jeremiah 17:7

Lesson #3: God's approval cannot be earned.

I imagine that Adam and Eve instantly lost confidence in their connection with the Father. As time wore on, they probably forgot what it felt like to live in the presence of God. Maybe they sat together at night and considered ways to win back God's approval. What could they do to feel closer to Him again? Maybe if they did more for Him, worked harder each day or stayed on their best behavior, they could get that old connection back.

Do you recognize the cycle: working to gain God's acceptance and approval by "being" and "doing" good, yet continually falling short?

In what ways have you bought into the lie that you have to perform a certain way in order to achieve God's approval?

Do you operate in the same performance-oriented acceptance in any of your other relationships? How have those relationships left you feeling?

Thankfully, God doesn't leave us to our own desperate attempts to please. Knowing our need for a different kind of heavenly clothing, God sent Jesus who came ready to cover us once and for all. Jesus didn't merely provide a worthy wardrobe. He became our covering. Through His perfect life and innocent bloodshed on the cross, Jesus gave us access to His Father once again. He stepped in and took our ugliness and our shame.

There's no need to work to win God's approval. Jesus has covered us completely. More than that, He invites us to wrap ourselves in Him each day. When we do like Romans 13:14 says – when we clothe ourselves with the Lord Jesus Christ – we're able to experience life as it was intended. Plan A: Garden Life.

We'll end this chapter with one last verse.

Read Galatians 5:1. Write it out in the space provided.

Jesus Christ has set you free! Free from a life controlled by thoughts and feelings. Free from your desperate attempts for independence. Free from the approval addiction. Free from working for your salvation. You are called to be free. Stand firm, then and exercise that freedom by living a life of faith!

CHAPTER 2

THE NEW YOU

Have you ever had a personal clothes fitting? In high school I had a dress made for a senior presentation. We all had to wear white but I didn't want my dress to look like I was getting married. I opted for a fancy, tailed suit. My second fitting was for my wedding dress, which looked decidedly bridal. For each fitting, fabric was pinned, pinched, tucked in and stitched so that the clothes fit just right. Each piece was tailored exclusively for me.

This chapter of the Bible study is going to be like a personal fitting by the Ultimate Tailor. My only request is that you go into the fitting with an open heart and mind. There is no "one size fits all" approach to a fitting. Each is unique and specific to the individual being sized. All along the way, allow the Holy Spirit to lead you as you assess your current spiritual wardrobe. Father God may have to do a little pinning, pinching, tucking and sticking, but in the end you'll be dressed in a whole new wardrobe.

DAY 1
PUT OFF THE OLD

Read Ephesians 4:22-24. Fill in the blanks below.

Verse 22: Put off _____

Verse 23: Be made new _____

Verse 24: Put on _____

Before we can properly dress each day, we have to take a few things off. As attractive as our pajamas may be, we don't keep them on all day long. We have to strip off our nightly wear in order to put on our daywear. The same is true when we are getting dressed spiritually. If we want to put on our new self, we need to put off our old self first. To do this, we must first understand the old self.

When we were born into this world, we were born into a family. With that family came a family history and a lineage. Trace the lines all the way back and you will find Adam. Therefore, our old self has the family resemblance of our first father, Adam.

Read Romans 5:12 and Romans 5:16. What are some of the things we have inherited from Adam?

It's important to know what the future has in store for our sinful nature. It isn't a pretty picture. Sin, judgment, condemnation, and death – not exactly the life we aspire to. That's the reality of our lives alienated from God.

The Bible also gives us an accurate portrait of the traits associated with the flesh.

Write down some of the other traits associated with our "old man." (Galatians 5:19-21, Colossians 3:5-9)

Try as we may, we can't deny that these traits fight to show their ugly heads in our lives when we live apart from God. We're rotten through and through. Corrupt to the core. However, we don't have to live that way. Paul tells us to put off, cast away, deny or lay down our old man. Like old clothes that we've thrown away, we're called to walk away from our old way of living and think of that old life no more.

What are some of the fleshly traits that you would like to throw off? How does your "old nature" try to show itself in your life?

Read Ephesians 4:22 again, this time from The Message:

"Since, then, we do not have the excuse of ignorance, everything—and I do mean everything—connected with that old way of life has to go. It's rotten through and through. Get rid of it!"

Have you ever seen the television show called *What Not To Wear*? In each episode, one person is nominated by a loved one to receive a total closet makeover. The only catch: they have to commit to throwing away their *entire* old wardrobe. Nothing stays. It all has to go. Much to the dismay of the on-looking fashion challenged participant, each article of clothing is thrown into the trash, hanger and all.

Now imagine your old self on *What Not To Wear*. If you agree to fully step into your new self, the entire old self has to go. Remember, the old self has no redeeming qualities. It is a slave to sin (Romans 6:6) and offers no hope of rehabilitation. But it's your choice to make. Are you willing to "put off" the old self? If so, grab the biggest trash can you can find and start dumping. Tomorrow we will be embarking on a God-sized transformation.

Spend the remainder of our time in prayer. Ask God to bring to mind any parts of the old self that you have not yet thrown away. Is there some part of the old you that you are unknowingly holding on to? Use the following verse as a guide.

"Search me, O God, and know my heart; test me and know my anxious thoughts. See if there is any offensive way in me, and lead me in the way everlasting." Psalm 139:23-24

DAY 2
THE GREAT EXCHANGE

Did you wake up this morning feeling lighter on your feet after yesterday's cleanout? There's nothing quite as freeing as a good old fashioned cleaning day. As a matter of fact, my husband knows the look in my eyes when I need to do some purging. No closet is safe when this mamma is in the mood to clean out and throw away!

Now that our old self has been taken off and hauled away, we can begin to focus on the new self. There are two kinds of change that happen in the life of every believer. The first is the conversion that occurs upon salvation. The second is the progressive transformation as we become more like Jesus.

For most of us, today's lesson will be a review of the foundations of our faith. I'm certain that there is no experience in our lives more profound than the moment of our conversion. Therefore, review or not, the message bears repeating.

To begin, reread Ephesians 4:22-24.

The moment we accept Jesus as our Lord and Savior, we are made new. The miraculous truth is that this "new" isn't a transformed new, like a caterpillar turning into a butterfly. The "new" this verse is referring to is brand new, a quality that never existed before. You and I are made new from the inside out; we are reborn.

When we allow Jesus to take control of our lives, He miraculously changes our identity. We are no longer enemies of God. Instead we are adopted into His family. We become children of God and co-heirs with Christ (Romans 8:17). What an amazing exchange!

Look up the following verses and fill in the table.

What we give up	Reference	What we get in return
Sin	2 Corinthians 5:21	The righteousness of God
Wrath of God	Romans 5:1	
Death	Romans 5:17	
Our Weakness	2 Corinthians 12:9-10	
Our Impurity	Hebrews 10:19-22	
Bondage	John 8:34-36	
Defeat	1 Corinthians 15:56-57	
Under Law	Romans 6:14	

The list could go on, but will you indulge me in looking up one more verse?

Write Galatians 2:20 in the space provided.

If you have not already, today is the day to "be made new in the attitude of your mind." If you have been born again, your old self has been crucified with Christ. Christ has changed your identity! It's no longer you who live, but Christ who lives in and through you. Take a moment and ask God to wash this miraculous truth over your mind in a fresh way.

Read Romans 12:2. Fill in the blanks.

"Do not _____ ... but be _____ by the_____of your _____."

As a written guideline for redeemed people in a fallen world, Paul tells us we should no longer allow the world to mold our character. Instead, we're commanded to renew our mind and be transformed. The word *transform* in this text is in the present tense, passive voice, and imperative mood. The present tense tells us that this is not a one-time event, like our conversion, but a continual process. The passive voice means that an outside force performs the transformation; it is not by our own power or strength. The imperative mood, however, indicates that we do have some responsibility in the process. So exactly what does transform mean?

Hold that thought and flip back to Matthew 17.

Read Matthew 17:1–5. Note what takes place.

Can you imagine the scene on the mountain that night? According to the Gospel of Luke, Peter, James and John were given the opportunity to get away with Jesus alone to pray. While praying, Jesus was transfigured before their eyes. Luke describes the transfiguration when he says, "the appearance of his face changed, and his clothes became as bright as a flash of lightning" (Luke 9:29). Mark says, "… His clothes became dazzling white, whiter than anyone in the world could bleach them" (Mark 9:3).

For a brief moment, the glory and majesty of Jesus shone through His garments so that His disciples could see His inner self manifested externally.

The same word transfiguration, or *metamorphoo,* is also translated as the word transformed in Romans 12:2. Thus, to be transformed describes a change on the *outside* that comes from the *inside.* Paul is calling for an outward change in the character and conduct, which is to correspond with our new inward spiritual condition.

How does that translate to you? Put into your words what it means to be transformed.

To me, transformation is evidence of God's hand upon my life. It is proof that He loves me too much to let me remain the way I am. God wants to see growth in my life. He also delights in participating in the miraculous change that causes me to look more like His son.

The great exchange we receive in Christ is our new reality. In Him, our lives are forever changed from the inside out. Spend the rest of your day basking in the amazing transforming power of our Heavenly Father. He is undoubtedly worthy of our praise!

DAY 3
RENEWING YOUR MIND

Yesterday we discovered the amazing truth about our transformation. By looking into the context of the word, we discovered that our transformation is an act of God which occurs upon our lives. It's His touch alone that changes us. However, we also learned that we do have some responsibility in the process.

Look back at Romans 12:2. Write down how we are to participate in the transformation process.

Even though we're new creations in Christ, our mind is still programmed with its old way of thinking. Although God is responsible for the process of change, we are accountable for our participation in the process.

The single most effective way we can participate in the renewing of our minds is by digging into God's Word. By reading, meditating on and memorizing the Word, God will begin to train us to become more like Him.

Before we discuss this more, we're going to look up some verses that relate to the power of God's word in our lives. Next to each verse, make note of what each reveals about the importance and power of God's word written on our hearts and minds.

Hebrews 4:12:

John 17:17:

Psalm 1:1-3:

Joshua 1:8:

Isaiah 55:11:

For the majority of my life I've struggled with memorizing scripture. No matter how much I tried, it seemed as though the skill of memorization had eluded me. A few years ago, I decided I wanted more. In quiet desperation, I begged God to give me a desire for His Word – for Him to light a flame in my heart for the Scriptures – and did He ever answer my request!

What about you? Is memorizing Scripture something you practice often? Why or why not? Have you considered asking God for a desire for His Word?

By the grace of God, He answered my prayers and gave me an insatiable desire to know Him through His powerful Word. In doing so, He also gave me the desire to participate in the work of training my mind.

Training our minds in God's Truth requires discipline and dedication. Have you taken the time to consider what you are letting into your mind? I'm a firm believer in the "garbage in/garbage out" mentality. If all we are absorbing into our minds is garbage, than we can expect the output to be the same. Conversely, if we are inundating our minds with Truth, Truth will become our output. We are affected by so many sources of external input. Television shows, commercials, movies, music, Internet, magazine, books … little by little our minds are being shaped by the noise around us. It takes discipline to focus our minds on only that which pleases the Father.

The Bible is clear about how we are to take an offensive stand when it comes to what enters our minds.

Read 2 Corinthians 10:5. Write down what we are to do with each thought that we process.

I love the military terms used here. We are to demolish (take down, destroy) and take captive (bring into captivity) every thought to the obedience of Christ. Ladies, that is the working definition of intentional thinking!

Let's picture how this works.

1. A thought comes into our minds.

2. "Hold that thought." Take it captive. Why? Because we need to make sure we are only allowing Truth to pass through the threshold of our minds. This step has to be intentional. Just as we don't let just anyone who approaches our door come into our homes, neither should we let every thought walk through the door of our minds.

3. Hold the thought up to the light of God's Word. Is it sound? Does it line up with the Truth of God's Word? If it does, then by all means let it in. If it doesn't, bind that thought up and throw it away. It has no place in the mind of a child of the King.

Can you see how important it is that we know what's lining the pages of our Bibles? When you take the time to wallpaper your mind with His Word, the Spirit of God will enable you to recognize Truth and decipher it from the lies.

Because God is good, He has also given some standards of thinking – a cheat sheet, if you will – of that which is acceptable to think on.

Read Philippians 4:8.

Instead of getting caught up in this long list of "whatever's", we're going to look at each word listed in this verse one at a time. I'll define each word and post a question to assist you in applying each one. As you read the list, use space provided to jot down any situation that comes to mind where you might need to put this list into practice. Please put a check mark in the box after you have read each and comprehended its meaning.

❑ **True: "whatever is actual, true to fact, conforming to reality"**

Ask yourself: Is this thought a fact or is it based on another thought or feeling? Is it an embellishment or a skewing of the facts?

❑ **Noble: "worthy of respect, entitled to honor, invokes an awe-inspiring respect"**

Ask yourself: Does this thought have honest value? Does it invite a sense of respect?

❑ **Right: "upright, just, keeping the commands of God, used of him whose way of thinking, feeling and acting is wholly conformed to the will of God"**

Ask yourself: Does that to which I am setting my mind to conform to the holiness of God? Does it satisfy merely my own standards or the ones set by God?

❑ **Pure: "free from defilement, stainless, that which will not contaminate, that which is "morally and inwardly" innocent"**

Ask yourself: Will this thought defile me? Will it corrupt my thinking if I give attention to it? Does is stand the scrutiny of God?

❑ **Lovely:** "acceptable, pleasing, pleasing in its motive and actions towards others"

Ask yourself: Will this thought produce peace or will giving attention to it produce strife?

❑ **Admirable:** "good report, commendable, well-spoken of"

Ask yourself: Am I concentrating on the good things I see in others or am I dwelling on their faults and imperfections?

❑ **Excellent:** "moral excellence – anything that properly fulfills its purpose, perfection, goodness of action"

Ask yourself: Will this thought hinder my growth in godliness?

❑ **Praiseworthy:** "act of expressing admiration and praise, applause, something worthy of being praised"[3]

Ask yourself: Is this thought worthy of praise?

Pretty good start, isn't it? Did any of these words and their meanings surprise you? If so, which ones and why?

Each word Paul included in this list of acceptable thoughts is a call to a deliberate and offensive action as we seek to renew our minds. Without getting overwhelmed by the enormity of this moment-by-moment, thought-by-thought call to action, ask the Holy Spirit to take the lead as you yield to His mind-blowing power.

DAY 4
THE NEW SELF

Now that we've taken off the old self and allowed the Lord to change our minds, it's time to start dressing in the new self.

2 Corinthians 5:17 says, "Therefore, if anyone is in Christ, he is a new creation; the old has gone, the new has come!" In Jesus Christ we have a brand new wardrobe. Now we are going to have to learn how to wear each piece.

What does Colossians 3:10 say we must do?

Each day we have a choice. Even though our old self is dead and gone, we can still choose to follow the patterns of that old self (our flesh), or we can choose to step into our new identity in Christ. 1 Corinthians 15:49 says, "Just as we have borne the likeness of the earthly man, so shall we bear the likeness of the man from heaven." We were made to resemble Christ. Each day we can choose to wrap ourselves in the traits of the Lord Jesus Christ.

The rest of this week we are going to be focusing on postures of the new self. We'll uncover two today.

#1: THE NEW SELF SETS ITS GAZE UPWARDS.

Read Colossians 3:2. Write the verse in the space provided.

According to the Greek text, when we set our minds on things above, we are to direct our minds to the heavens. We are to seek and to strive for a heavenly perspective. Here are a couple of examples of how we can choose to live with our gaze upwards.

1. We are to seek God and His Kingdom as our first priority.

    "But seek first his kingdom and his righteousness, and all these things will be given to you as well." Matthew 6:33

    Have you noticed that on this side of heaven, there's a never-ending battle for position No. 1 on our priority lists? According to the previous verse, what should be our first priority?

27

Now open your daily planner or calendar. (Go ahead, I'll wait). Does your time reflect the same priority? If not, ask God how He would have you re-arrange your day to reflect that which you most highly esteem.

2. We live to please the Father in heaven.

"So we make it our goal to please Him, whether we are at home in the body or away from it. For we must all appear before the judgment seat of Christ, that each one may receive what is due him for the things done while in the body, whether good or bad." 2 Corinthians 5:9-10

There will be a day when all believers will stand before Jesus – not in judgment for our sin, that's already been taken care of – but to hold us accountable for the way that we lived. Are you really living with *that* day in mind? Here are a couple of questions to consider:

Are you a good steward of that which He has given you or are you wasting your life on worthless things? (Anything that lacks eternal significance will be burned away).

Do you know what your spiritual gifts are? Are you using your gifts for His name and fame or your own?

Are you making your time count? Are the things you are committed to of value to God's Kingdom?

Are you willing to invest your time, energy and resources for the sake of others instead of merely promoting self-interest?

When we approach the throne of Jesus, there's no time for second chances. Our life is but a mere blink on the eternal calendar. Are we using what little time we have to please the Father?

#2: THE NEW SELF LEARNS TO SETTLE INTO ITS HIDING PLACE.

Read Colossians 3:3. Write it in the space provided.

Here are three benefits of having a life that is hidden in Christ.

1. God is our ultimate hideout.

Is there ever a time in your day when you wish you could get away? As a stay-at-home mom of three, there are definitely moments when I wish I could clock out so I could regroup, refresh or unwind. That's when the truth of this verse comes into play. Our refuge, our hiding place, our sanctuary is always with us and promises to keep us safely tucked away. Peace is found when we learn to remain in that place with Him.

Practically speaking, how is Jesus a refuge for you?

2. The source of our lives is hidden with Christ in God.

J.R. Miller gives a picturesque example that beautifully illustrates the concept of God as the source of our lives.

> "Outside an old garden wall hung a great branch covered with purple clusters of grapes. No root was visible anywhere; and those who saw it wondered how the vine grew, how its life was nourished, where its roots clung. It was then discovered that the great vine from which this branch sprung, grew inside the garden. There it had an immense root, with a stem like the trunk of a tree. This one branch had pushed out over the wall and hung there, bearing in the mellow autumn its clusters of luscious fruit.
>
> Likewise every Christian life in this world is a branch of a great vine which grows in heaven—a branch growing outside the wall. "Your life is hidden with Christ in God." We have heaven's life in us in this world. The fruits which grow upon our life are heavenly fruits.
>
> Thus in our human experience in this world—we are drawing our life and its support from the hidden source of life which is in the heart of God. This assures us of its security. It is beyond the reach of earthly harm."[4]

3. We have access to everything that is also hidden with Jesus.

What else is hidden with Jesus? In Colossians 2:3 Paul names Christ as the one "in whom are hidden all the treasures of wisdom and knowledge." Tucked away with Jesus is the storehouse of wisdom and knowledge. The mother-load, as some might call it. Hide away with Jesus and you will be given access to the treasures of the King of Kings. What a promise!

Learning to live in the new self is a life-long journey. The transformation doesn't happen in an instant and it doesn't happen by accident. The more you and I practice walking in the new self, the more we will realize it is who we were made to be.

DAY 5
THE LIGHT OF THE WORLD

Yesterday we discussed two postures of our new self.

List the first two postures of the new self.

#1:

#2:

Today we're going to close the week with one more quality of the new self.

Read Ephesians 5:8. Check the boxes that apply.

❑ **You were once in darkness**
❑ **You were once darkness**
❑ **Now you are in the light of the Lord**
❑ **Now you are light in the Lord**

I know it seems picky, but the lack of one little word makes a huge difference in each sentence. Before Christ, we were not in darkness; we were darkness. Ouch! However, with Christ – because of Christ – in Christ – through Christ (are you catching on that it's all because of Christ living inside us), we *are* light. Amazing!

I love the end of the Ephesians 5:8, "Live as children of light." The Amplified version says, "Lead the lives of those native-born to the Light." Paul reminds us that our new position in Christ does not guarantee that we will live as "children of light" consistently. He makes no promise that we will always feel light worthy. Instead, Paul commands us to live in a way that is consistent with our character as a redeemed child of God.

Read Matthew 5:14-16. Fill in the blanks below.

"You are the _____ of the _____."

When I was in high school, our youth group bravely occupied the front few rows of the sanctuary during the Sunday morning late service. I will never forget one song that we sang as a congregation. I can't recall the song in its entirety, but one line of the chorus stands out as clear as day: "Carry the Light. Carry the Light." Being that my name is Carrie, the guys around me would sing as if they were serenading me, "Carrie – the light. Carrie – the light." I loved it! Being a light-bearer was and is an honor to me, and I reveled in the title that they attached to my name.

Biblically speaking, however, the title is not mine alone to claim. You too are a light. So, go ahead and sing your song too.

"_____ (Insert your name) – the light. _____ - the light".

Now read the text in Matthew5:14-16 again, but this time from The Message.

"Here's another way to put it: You're here to be light, bringing out the God-colors in the world. God is not a secret to be kept. We're going public with this, as public as a city on a hill. If I make you light-bearers, you don't think I'm going to hide you under a bucket, do you? I'm putting you on a light stand. Now that I've put you there on a hilltop, on a light stand—shine! Keep open house; be generous with your lives. By opening up to others, you'll prompt people to open up with God, this generous Father in heaven."

I love the way God calls us out in this verse. He says (paraphrased), "Now don't you go thinking that you can hide MY light under a bucket. I made you to shine!" Unfortunately there are "lights" all around us that are covered up, hiding. Maybe it's us. Maybe we are the ones with buckets on our heads, hindering our shine-ability.

I believe there are two predominate ways we hide our ability to shine.

#1: SIN. When a light bulb is dirty, the light is dimmed. Simply put: unconfessed sin makes our light bulbs dirty – sometimes too dirty to see the light at all.

#2: FEAR. "Fear of what" you might say? Fear of what others will think, fear of what they might say to you or about you, fear of how you will be received, fear of losing someone because of how you shine or how your shine affects those around you.

Where do you think you fall on the shine-o-meter? Rate yourself from 1 to 10. (1 = Your light is completely covered up, 10 = Your light is glowing for all the world to see)

What do you think affects your light's ability to shine the most? Is it unconfessed sin or fear that masks your bulb? What are you going to do about it now?

The verse then goes on to say that we have all been given a lamp stand – a place to set our lights for the entire world to see. Many analogies have been given to create a picture of believers as light bearers.

Which dispenser of light do you picture when considering how you shine?

❑ **A candle with a flickering glow**

- ❏ **An oil burning lamp**
- ❏ **A light bulb attached to a light switch**
- ❏ **A lighthouse with an ever probing light**
- ❏ **A campfire glow**

Explain why.

The best analogy I've heard is that we resemble the light of a solar lamp. These light-bearers are solely powered by light from the sun. The amount of energy absorbed each day in the form of light is directly proportional to the amount of light they transmit. Try as it may, the little light has nothing to emit if it's spent no time in the sun.

You see where I'm going with this, don't you? We are exactly like solar lamps. The only light we have to bear is the light we have received from the Son. Our responsibility in shining is only to stay as close as we can to the source. We have no means to shine on our own.

Think about the people in your life that seem to glow brightly. What is it about them that makes them shine so brilliantly?

Good work this week, my friend. The foundations we have set these first two chapters have prepared us for what lies ahead. From here on we will be focusing on the traits that wardrobe the life of Jesus Christ.

CHAPTER 3

COMPASSION AND KINDNESS

We all have a style of clothes that we are comfortable in, clothes that we think represent who we are. When I wake up each day, I put on clothes that look like me. You can be sure I won't be wearing many pastel colored blouses with lace and bows. That's just not me! I'm more of a simple T-shirt and jeans girl.

Spiritually speaking, as we dress each day there are traits that we can put on to make us look more like Jesus. What does this new self look like? We're going to be camping for a while in Colossians, so grab your Bible, a cup of something yummy to drink (I'm thinking coffee – hot and heavily sweetened), and let's dig in!

DAY 1
CHOSEN, HOLY AND DEARLY LOVED

Read Colossians 3:12-14 … our primary text for the remainder of the study.

Remember last week when we talked about wallpapering our minds with the Word of God? Well, no time like the present to start memorizing. Grab a note card and write out the verse in its entirety. Once again, I'm using the NIV translation, but you can memorize it in whatever translation you prefer. Place the card where you will see it every day – like on your bathroom mirror where you get dressed each day. Read it out loud and practice reciting it throughout your day.

Now write verse 12 below.

Paul makes some assumptions about what we should already know about ourselves as believers in Christ.

According to Colossians 3:12, what are the three descriptive words Paul uses?

1. CHOSEN

The word "chosen" in the text is translated as "the elect of God, picked out by God." The first thing that comes to mind when I think of a "chosen child" is adoption.

Read Ephesians 1:4-5.

By the grace of God, before the foundations of the world, you and I were picked out by God to be a part of His family. We are adopted children of the King. I don't know about you, but that fact stuns me. God, the One who sees me and knows every tiny detail about me, chose me for Himself. He didn't choose me because I deserve it or because I am good enough to be called one of His own. No. He chose me because of His great love for me. When you and I came into this world, I imagine God leaning over to Jesus saying, "You see that little one there? That one is ours. She's one of our chosen ones."

By adopting us, our Heavenly Father invites us to participate in life as part of His royal family. Do you realize that in God's eyes, you are royalty? Have you pondered the privilege you have to be counted as a member of God's royal family?

Sadly, many of us lose sight of our position as a chosen child of the Lord, so we turn to the world to satisfy our needs to feel wanted. Just as each situation provides the opportunity to feel "chosen," it equally sets us up for rejection.

In each box below, put a check mark next to the situation in which you experienced the thrill of being chosen or an 'X' over the box when you experienced rejection.

- ❑ **Chosen for the team**
- ❑ **Chosen to be first**
- ❑ **Chosen by the boy**
- ❑ **Chosen to be in the "in" crowd**
- ❑ **Chosen for the part**
- ❑ **Chosen for the position**
- ❑ **Chosen for the promotion**
- ❑ _____ **(fill in the blank)**

It's true, the world provides many opportunities to be a "chosen one," but all pale in comparison to living as the chosen of God.

Read 1 Peter 2:9.

The Amplified Bible translates the verse in this way:

"But you are a chosen race, a royal priesthood, a dedicated nation, [God's] own purchased, special people, that you may set forth the wonderful deeds and display the virtues and perfections of Him who called you out of darkness into His marvelous light."

According to the previous verse, what are our two purposes as chosen children?

1.

2.

His name and His fame: that's what it's all about. Paul uses one more descriptive phase in this verse that I want to briefly touch on. He calls us a "royal priesthood." Ever tagged that phrase to your earthy job description?

In the Old Testament times, people could not approach God directly. A priest served as the intermediary between God and His fallen race. With Christ's victory on the cross, that pattern changed. Now we can come directly into God's presence without fear, and we are given the responsibility of bringing others to Him. When we are united with Christ, we join in his priestly work of reconciling God and man.[5]

Name one way you could live your life differently in the knowledge of this truth?

2. HOLY

The second word Paul uses to describe a believer is "holy."

Read the following verses. Connect each verse to its corresponding truth.

Hebrews 10:10	A holy root produces holy branches.
Romans 11:16	I am called to be holy because Jesus is holy.
1 Peter 1:15-16	I have been made holy through the sacrifice of Jesus

Think back to our lesson on the Great Exchange: we relinquish all that we are that we might receive all that He is. In doing so, Christ becomes our holiness. The word holy in this text is defined as "consecrated and set apart for him, sharing in God's purity and abstaining from the earth's defilement."

To understand the concept of our holiness in Christ, consider your china dinnerware or crystal stemware. If you are like most people, you have these valuable and fragile pieces stored away, out of reach from everyday use. You have set them apart for special occasions. In the same way, God has set you and me apart from the corrupt ways of the world in order that we might serve and worship our Most Holy God. God has set us apart for His special purposes.

God calls us to be holy – to be morally upright and blameless in our conduct – just as He is holy. Sound impossible? Genesis 17:1 says, "When Abram was ninety-nine years old, the Lord appeared to him and said, 'I am God Almighty; walk before me and be blameless.'" So the question stands: Does God ever command us to do something that's impossible?

Yes … and no. Yes – God commands us to behave and live our lives in ways that are far beyond our capabilities. It's impossible for you and me to be holy and blameless by our own merit. (See John 15:5) However, God never asks us to live our lives by our own merit. Can we live blameless lives? Absolutely. "For nothing is impossible with God." (Luke 1:37) As we live out our lives in the presence of the Father, Jesus can live a holy and blameless life through you and me. Once again, it's a picture of the Great Exchange: His life for ours.

3. DEARY LOVED

The last phrase used to describe every child of God is "dearly loved." It is defined as, "to be fond of, to be well pleased by God Himself, favorite, worthy of love." Just as you are the chosen of God and set apart for His glory, you are also one of His favorites, the apple of His eye.

Write Ephesians 5:1 in the space provided.

If you have children, you know what it means to be imitated. As soon as my first daughter could walk, she had a purse on her shoulder and a cell phone in her hand. She loved to act like mommy. The more kids I have had, the more I see my husband and me all over the little things they say and do. They imitate us because they are our dearly loved children. What amazes me most are the ways they imitate us without knowing it. Just because they are mine, my children bear resemblances of my husband and me. It's in their DNA. From the shape and color of their eyes to their round little cheeks to the curl of their toes, our children look like the ones who conceived them.

As dearly loved children of our Heavenly Father, we are called to be imitators of Him. Do we mimic Him in our behavior? Do we bear resemblances of Him in our thoughts and attitudes? Do people look at us and say, "Wow! You remind me so much of your Father!?"

Paul assumes that we, as believers, know these three fundamental truths about ourselves. You and I are chosen, holy and dearly loved.

Do you believe that to be true? If no, which of the three do you struggle with most? Why?

As you move through your day, let your mind mull over the truths in our lesson today. You are chosen – you are holy – you are dearly loved. Soak it in and believe it's true. You are God's favorite!

DAY 2
COMPASSION

Read Colossians 3:12-14. Remember, repetition is the key to inscribing God's Word on your heart and mind.

Allow me to recap what we talked about yesterday by paraphrasing Paul's assumptions. He says, "Because you *know* that you are chosen by God, called according to his good purpose and loved beyond reason – because you *know* that you are in Christ and that by the power of the cross and the Holy Spirit living inside of you, you have been made holy – because you have realized, absorbed and become comfortable in your new skin … clothe yourself."

According to Colossians 3:12, what is the first trait that we are to put on?

_____

The word used for compassion in this text is actually translated "the heart of compassion" or "the bowels of mercies." This compassion, *oiktirmos* in Greek, is defined as "a sympathetic consciousness of other's distress together with a desire to alleviate it." Biblical compassion is a deep-seated emotion that comes from what we often call "the pit of your stomach." It is a type of caring that goes beyond feeling pity for someone.

Before we begin our journey following the thread of compassion woven through out the Word, I want to deal with an old pattern of the flesh that may be lurking in the background.

What is the first thing you think of when you hear the word compassion?

If you are like me, all this compassion talk sounds a little too warm and fuzzy. If so, this one is for you.

Read Ezekiel 36:26. Fill in the blanks below.

"…I will remove from you your _____ of _____ and give you a _____ of _____ …"

I love this verse because I can really relate to it. Sometimes I feel like I have a heart of stone. I don't have a sugary sweet personality. Sometimes when I compare myself to those with softer dispositions, I feel the heavy weight of a stone in my chest. However I know that's not the truth. When I stepped into my new self, a new heart came with it: a heart full of God's loving compassion.

Read Psalm 103:4. List the two benefits of the Lord stated in this verse.

The Greek word for "crowns" is *atar* meaning, "to grant honor, protect and surround." God places love and compassion on us as a symbol of honor. It literally surrounds and protects us. By allowing the spirit of God to move and breathe through us, we can exude the sweet aroma of compassion to the hurting world around us. By his tender mercies, Christ's heart will bestow compassion through you and me. Remember, it's no longer what we look like, but what Christ looks like living in and through us. It's a perfect picture of great exchange: our lack of sensitivity for His compassion.

Back to our thread of compassion …

Read Exodus 34:4-7.

Enter the story of Moses and the Ten Commandments. After God engraved the Ten Commandments on the tablets of stone, Moses headed down the mountain to deliver the Law to his people. When he arrived, the Israelites were caught red handed with an idol of gold. In his fury Moses threw the tablets, which consequently broke into pieces. Later God, who is rich in mercy, directed Moses back up the mountain where the Ten Commandments were written again.

What did Moses ask of God in Exodus 33:18?

Instead, God told Moses of his character.

How did he describe himself? (Exodus 34:6)

God could have showed Moses His power and majesty, but instead He showed him His heart. He does the same for you and me.

Describe a time in your life when God revealed His tender compassions to you.

There are many stories of our compassionate God pouring out unmerited favor on His children.

We'll close today by looking up the following verses. List some of the ways God has blessed His people.

Nehemiah 9:16-21

Psalm 103:8-10

Ephesians 2:4-7

Titus 3:4-7

Slow to anger and abounding in love and compassion. We are blessed indeed.

DAY 3
THE FATHER OF COMPASSION

Begin by reading 2 Corinthians 1:3-4.

In his second letter to the church in Corinth, Paul begins by giving praise to God by using two distinct titles:

1. Father of compassion: By using the term "father," Paul is naming God the originator of compassion, which is also translated as mercies. All compassion and mercy begins with God. He also uses the title "father" to show God's relationship with us. As our Heavenly Father, God operates only out of compassion with His children. He cares deeply about our lives and is filled with compassion for us (James 5:11).

2. God of all comfort: Comfort is defined as, "a calling to one's side, either a consolation or exhortation." Picture God standing by your side with His ever-present hand on your shoulder. Comfort doesn't mean that God's going to take your suffering away. Instead, God comforts you by providing strength, hope, encouragement and the promise of His presence as you walk through your suffering.

God is rich in compassion and mercy. Each and every time you are looking for comfort, God is ready and able to supply it. He doesn't just give you *a little* or *some* comfort. He gives you *all* the comfort you need *every* time you need it. He is the Father of Compassion and the God of *all* comfort.

Truth be told, I don't always look to God for my comfort. It's not that I forget that He's there. I just choose to look for something tangible to comfort me. I want instant gratification in my time of need. What "other" do you go to for comfort? Is it food, alcohol, a person, shopping, exercise or isolation? The list of vices may change and there are many to choose from, but the reality is always the same. Each is at best a counterfeit comforter, a temporary bandage and a worthless substitute compared to the God of all comfort.

What or who do you usually turn to when you need comfort? Why?

God wants to be your comfort all of the time. Not just when you hit rock bottom. Not just when the test results come back positive. Not just when you're all alone. He wants to be there to comfort you each time you need it, for the big things and the small. Lamentations 3:22-23 says, "Because of the Lord's great love we are not consumed, for his compassions never fail. They are new every morning; great is your faithfulness." Each morning God has waiting for you all the compassion and mercy you need for the day. It's yours for the taking. No need to run to substitute comforters. You have the real thing at your disposal. Go to God. Ask for your fill. He'll never let you down.

Can you look back at a time in your life when you knew that you experienced the comfort and compassion of God? Briefly describe what you experienced.

When I look back at my life, my memories attest to the faithfulness of God. Though I've experienced times of darkness and periods of time when I didn't know where He was, God has never let me down. Not once. Each barren season of winter has always been followed by the new life of spring. Each dark night yielded to the bright morning light. God is faithful. He's always with us, there to comfort in our time of need.

So, how does God comfort His children?

#1: THE HOLY SPIRIT

Read John 14:16-17.

The word "counselor" is also translated helper, advocate, encourager and comforter. The spirit of truth or the Holy Spirit was sent to be our personal comforter. By living inside each believer, the Holy Spirit comforts us by teaching us, leading us and giving us peace (John 14:26-27). He's God's inside-out approach to showing compassion and comfort to His children.

#2: GOD'S WORD

Read Psalm 119:49-52 and Romans 15:4. According to theses verses, how are we comforted by God's Word?

The Bible was written as a source of comfort to its readers. God uses each story told and each command given to comfort us in our times of need. Psalm 119 is filled with verses about how we find comfort and protection within the boundaries that God has given us throughout His Word. This living and active Word has the supernatural ability to speak straight to our hearts by encouraging us and giving us hope.

#3: OTHER BELIEVERS

Read the following verses written below.

"Therefore encourage one another and build each other up, just as in fact you are doing." 1 Thessalonians 5:11

"All praise to the God and Father of our Master, Jesus the Messiah! Father of all mercy! God of all healing counsel! He comes alongside us when we go through hard times, and before you know it, he brings us alongside someone else who is going through hard times so that we can be there for that person just as God was there for us." 2 Corinthians 1:3-4 MSG

Often times when God comforts you, He intends to use you to comfort another. In turn, He channels his comfort through you and me.

Writer Anne LaMotte says that the most powerful sermon in the world is two words: "Me Too."

"Me too. When you're struggling, when you are hurting, wounded, limping, doubting, questioning, barely hanging on, moments away from another relapse, and somebody can identify with you – someone knows the temptations that are at your door, somebody has felt the pain that you are feeling, when someone can look you in the eyes and say, "Me too", and they actually mean it – it can save you."[6]

Prayer is the single most powerful way we can comfort others in their time of need. Paul, in his letter to the church in Colosse, gives a great prayer to model how we are to pray for others.

Read Colossians 1:9-12. Based on this verse, jot down some ways we can pray for each other.

When you've walked the same road as your neighbor, you can understand and sympathize with their need like no one else. Being on the other side of the trial, you know the need for God's guidance, strength and hope to make it through. As you offer your shoulder to cry on and your listening ear let God use you to bestow His comfort and compassion as you lift others up in prayer.

DAY 4
PORTRAITS OF KINDNESS

We are going to start today by reading our main text in Colossians.

According to Colossians 3:12, what's the second trait we are to put on?

Read Jeremiah 9:23-24.

When God speaks to us through His Word, He tells it like it is. Doesn't He? God says, "You want to boast about something. How about this: boast about the fact that you know me – that you have a personal and practical relationship with me – that you really know my character and what I'm all about" (Amplified Bible).

According to the text, what is the first word God uses to describe Himself?

The word kindness used here is the Hebrew word *checed,* which is a word rich in meaning. Depending on what translation of the Bible you carry, the word could also read loving kindness, unfailing love, loyal love, mercy or faithfulness. This word for "kindness" is way more than just being nice to someone. It's based on the covenant love of our Heavenly Father.

Way back in Genesis, God called Abram, later re-named Abraham, to follow Him. When he did, God initiated a covenant between Himself and Abraham. This covenant, or promise, was an oath of loyalty and love to one another. Once made, God promised to show His love to Abraham and to a thousand generations of those who love Him and keep His commands (Exodus 20:6). Loving kindness, therefore, is a picture of that covenant love at work.

In order to fully understand the act of kindness, I want to walk you through a couple stories in the Old Testament. I will refrain from adding narration as you read. I think you will find that these stories of old will speak for themselves.

RAHAB

Read Joshua 2:1-14. What was Rahab's occupation?

Why do you think that Rahab's house was a good place for the spies to hide?

❑ It was a good place for them to ask questions without looking suspicious.
❑ It was in an ideal location for a quick escape because it was built into the city wall.
❑ God directed the spies there because He knew Rahab's heart was open to him and that she would be instrumental in the Israelite victory over Jericho.
❑ All of the above.

Why did she choose to show the men kindness and hide them from the King's men?

What did she ask for in return for her kindness?

There are many things that could have held Rahab back from extending kindness to the spies, but she counted the cost and took the risk.

DAVID

Read 1 Samuel 20:12-17. What was the covenant made between David and Jonathan?

How long was the covenant to last?

Who does Jonathan reference as the perfect example of kindness (verse 14)?

Read 2 Samuel 9:1-13. Why did David call for Mephibosheth?

Read 2 Samuel 4:4. Who is Mephibosheth? How did he become cripple?

How did David show kindness to Mephibosheth?

Do you see how David said he was looking to show God's kindness to someone in Saul's family? He was intentional about his desire to extend the heart of God to those around him in need.

Your last exercise for today will be to look up these last few references for the Hebrew word *checed*. Note what each teaches about kindness. Remember the word kindness may be disguised as the words "love", "faithful", "unfailing love", "enduring love", or "mercy".

Psalm 25:10

Psalm 26:3

Psalm 32:10

Micah 6:8

After reading the two stories and the verses above, what have you learned about kindness in the Old Testament? Share your thoughts.

Throughout the Old Testament, kindness is used interchangeably with some of the most descriptive character traits of our Heavenly Father. God's kindness towards His children is linked to His unfailing love, His enduring faithfulness and His tender mercies. Put together like a beautifully wrapped package, these traits perfectly portray the heart of God.

Spend the rest of the day meditating on these newfound concepts about kindness. Ask the Lord to open the eyes of your heart so that you might gain a better understanding and view of your Father in Heaven.

DAY 5
KINDNESS

Yesterday we spent our time studying the Hebrew word for kindness used in the Old Testament.

Can you remember some of the words used interchangeably with kindness? If so, list them.

How does the covenant love of God that propelled acts of kindness in the Old Testament carry over to New Testament believers?

Read Galatians 3:26-29. Fill in the missing words.

"If you _____to_____, then you are _____'s seed, and _____ according to the _____." (Verse 29)

The God Abraham worshiped in the Old Testament is the same God we praise today. His promises still remain true. If you belong to Christ, it's your "birth right" to hold fast to covenant love and faithfulness of Your God.

Now read Ephesians 2:6-7 and Titus 3:4-7.

Our salvation and redemption is based entirely on the kindness and love of the Father. His kindness, spoken in the form of a covenant thousands of years ago, reached a crescendo when Jesus hung on the cross. By His grace and mercy and because of His everlasting faithfulness, you and I now live under the umbrella of the kindness of God through our Lord and Savior, Jesus Christ.

The word "kindness" used in the New Testament is the word *chrestotes* meaning, "moral goodness or benevolence in action, good, useful." Here, kindness is best understood as compassion with hands and feet. It's the action behind that deep sense of sympathy towards others. Every kind act of God was prompted by His deep compassion for His children.

Jesus was driven by this same heart of compassion; like father, like son. The pages of the New Testament are filled with stories of Jesus being moved by compassion and extending a hand of kindness to others.

Take a look at some of the stories of Jesus extending a hand of kindness. Next to each, note what caused Jesus to get involved and what He did in response.

Matthew 14:13-14

Matthew 15:32-38

Mathew 20:29-34

In each of these stories, how did Jesus encounter those who needed His help? Check the boxes that apply.

☐ **He went out of His way looking for them.**
☐ **He came across them along His way.**
☐ **He answered a "help wanted" add.**

Jesus didn't have to go out of His way to come across someone in need. They were all around Him. He simply kept His heart and eyes open. Jesus was never put off or distracted by the hurting people. Even though He was often on His way, He was willing to put a pause in His plans to pursue a higher purpose.

What about you? When you see someone who is hurting, what do you do? Do you run the other direction or do you reach out a loving hand of compassion to those in need? Are you willing to get your hands dirty for the sake of someone else's pain?

When was the last time you were willing to be vulnerable and maybe even a little uncomfortable to help out someone in need? Tell us about it.

Where are the places you travel each day? In the space provide, list five places you frequent each day/week (It could be a school, an office building, a certain store, a coffee house, etc.)

In those places and all along the way are hurting people who are desperate for a glimpse of the heart of God. Ask the Holy Spirit to open your eyes and stir up your heart to those around you. Remember, Jesus didn't have to go out of His way to show kindness and neither do you. Kindness is at its best when it happens along the way.

Before we close our day, I'd like to bring this closer to home. Actually, today's the day that we're going to swing wide the doors of our homes in order to do a kindness inspection.

Before we begin, rite the definition of kindness again. Remember, biblical kindness is way more than just "being nice" to someone.

Read Titus 2:4-5 and Proverbs 31:26.

As women, we're instructed to be kind. In our homes, we're called to extend the heart of God to our family. Kindness should be a motivating force behind all of our behavior.

The reality of this truth is convicting to me - so convicting that God had me stop writing this chapter for almost two months so that I could practice what I'm preaching. When I began studying, I had no concept of the complexity of kindness. It was just being nice to me. Now I understand better why kindness is only operated by the power of the Holy Spirit (Galatians 5:22). I need the heart of God to move in me in order to live out compassion through kindness.

Spend some time thinking about what kindness looks like within the four walls of your home … and beyond. Do you show understanding and sympathy to those in your care? Are you gentle with them? Do you show them grace and mercy when they fail or let you down? What does (or could) kindness look like:

With your family?

And beyond … with those you interact with most (co-workers, friends, etc.)?

We will end this week in Proverbs.

Read Proverbs 3:3-4. Fill in the blanks.

"Let _____ and _____ never leave you; _____ them around your neck, _____ them on the tablet of your heart. Then you will win favor and a good name in the sight of God and man."

Did you guess that the first blank that probably reads "love" is also the same word for *kindness*. The Proverb commands that you and I are never to let kindness leave us. Like a necklace that falls to rest just above your heart, fasten kindness on each day… for then we will win favor and a good name in the sight of God and man.

The heart of compassion, a hand offered in kindness – these are the garments that wardrobe our lives when we clothe ourselves with Jesus. It could be a smile, a kind word, an invitation to lunch or an offer to help – small acts of kindness that extend the love of our Heavenly Father to a lost and dying world.

CHAPTER 4

HUMILITY

Before we dive in to this next chapter, I'm having a really difficult time putting to words the enormity of the command before us. It's beyond huge to me. Saint Augustine can do better than I. He said, "If you plan to build a tall house of virtues, you must first lay deep foundations of humility."

You know those days when you are running out the door and all you have time to put on before you leave is a little lip gloss and mascara. This is what we're talking about. If I may break this down to its simplest form, humility is our lip-gloss and mascara.

DAY 1
SELFLESS

"Therefore, as God's chosen people, holy and dearly loved, clothe yourselves with compassion, kindness, humility, gentleness and patience." Colossians 3:12

Listed smack dab in the middle of this verse, humility stands apart to me as the most beautiful garment worn by our Lord and Savior.

Define humility in your own words.

Humility, *tapeinophrosune* in Greek, is defined as, "a deep sense of one's moral littleness, lowliness of mind." Humility is an attitude. It's the way you perceive yourself in relation to others, specifically towards God. Humility isn't something we stumble into by accident. It's a virtue we are commanded to pursue – something we must consciously put on by the grace of God.

In the Old Testament, humility most often referred to how people related to Father God. However, Jesus took humility to a completely new level when He taught the horizontal dimension of this virtue. He says, "… learn from me, for I am gentle and humble in heart …" (Matthew 11:29). If we want to look like Jesus, we must learn from His example and adorn ourselves with humility. Andrew Murray, in his book *Humility* writes, "Christ is the humility of God embodied in human nature. He is eternal love humbling itself, clothing itself in the garb of meekness and gentleness, to win and serve and save us."[7]

Read Philippians 2:1-11.

From the start of Philippians 2, Paul commands us to once again act according to our new identity. Paraphrasing verses 1-2 he says, "If you are in Christ – if you have allowed Him to reside and reign in your heart – and if you have begun to enjoy some of the benefits of Jesus' presence in your life – any comfort in His love, fellowship with the Spirit, tenderness and compassion from the Father – then begin to live like Him."

Every part of Jesus' life was covered in humility.

Read Philippians 2:5. According to this verse, what about Jesus should we emulate?

The word for attitude is *phroneo* meaning, "to have the same mind, the same understanding, and the same bend." We're to take on a new natural bend – the bend of Jesus. By studying the life of Jesus, we can begin to understand what this "bend" actually looks like.

There are four actions that characterize the humble heart of Jesus. Today we'll discover the first. The other three will be covered in the days to come.

#1: SELFLESS

Philippians 2:6-7 says, "Who, being in very nature God, did not consider equality with God something to be grasped, but made himself nothing…."

I love this verse in the Amplified version. It reads, "Who, although being essentially one with God and in the form of God [possessing the fullness of the attributes which make God God], did not think this equality with God was a thing to be eagerly grasped or retained."

Jesus, like God, has always existed. Before time began and the world was formed, Jesus has been part of the eternal Godhead. John 1:1-3 says, "In the beginning was the Word, and the Word was with God, and the Word was God. He was in the beginning with God. All things came into being by Him, and apart from Him nothing came into being that has come into being."

However, Jesus didn't selfishly cling to His favored position as the Son of God. He let it go and in doing so forfeited His heavenly rights and authority for a time so that He could claim the redemption of fallen man. It was the most extravagant – most selfless thing He could do for a creation that He loved beyond all reason. He commands us to do the same.

Read Philippians 2:3-4. Fill in the blanks below.

Do _____ out of selfishness or pride but in _____ consider others better than yourself.

Selfishness is an earthly epidemic. We're all sick with it. We want what we want – we want it our way – and we usually want it now! Humility, however, is the opposite of selfishness. It's always selfless and others-focused.

Read the following verses. Note what each says about selfishness.

2 Timothy 3:1-2

Romans 15:1-3

Philippians 2:21

Isaiah 56:11

The path that Jesus took paved the way for a different kind of living. His life displayed the beauty and power of selflessness. Deferring to others, esteeming others, promoting others – the life that Jesus lived was marked by His humble heart towards His Father in Heaven *and* His fellow man.

So what's the cure for this disease of self-centeredness?

Read the following verses. List how we're to unlearn this earthly attitude of selfishness.

Matthew 16:24

2 Corinthians 5:15

Psalm 119:36

Romans 12:10 says, "Be devoted to one another in brotherly love. Honor one another above yourselves." The word honor means, "to value, esteem." To honor someone is to make them look good; it is to cheer them on to success; it is to put aside my plans, desires and personal gain in order to take the lead in promoting someone else's gain.

How do we put ourselves aside and prefer one another? Can you think of three practical ways you can "consider others better than yourself?"

1.

2.

3.

Selfishness is an enemy to unity and harmony.

Read James 3:13-18. Check each statement that applies to the text.

❑ **Humility comes from wisdom.**
❑ **Selfishness is earthly, unspiritual and motivated by the devil.**
❑ **Where there is selfishness you will find disorder and every kind of evil.**

Before we close for the day, note the four steps that we all take in progressing from selfish to selfless:

1. You want the spotlight for yourself.
2. You are willing to share the spotlight with someone else.
3. You delight when others are in the spotlight instead of you.
4. Your aim or goal is for others to be in the spotlight.

What step are you on?

Jesus wants us all to progress from step one to step four. He wants us all to honor one another above ourselves.[8]

Let's face it: we like for everything to be all about "me". After all, we're our own favorite leading ladies. We think about ourselves, look at ourselves and talk about ourselves all the time. It's time for a change! The more we defer to others, look out for their well-being and interests and put them above ourselves, the more we resemble Jesus Christ. As we imitate Him, we please Him. Nothing looks better on us than that!

DAY 2:
SACRIFICE

Yesterday we talked about the first act of humility: selflessness. Today we will discover the second. We're going to begin right where we left off.

Read Philippians 2:6-8 written below.

"Who, being in very nature God, did not consider equality with God something to be grasped, but made himself nothing, taking the very nature of a servant, being made in human likeness. And being found in appearance as a man, he humbled himself and became obedient to death – even death on a cross!"

Jesus made Himself nothing. Take just a second to think about that. He emptied Himself, laid aside His privileges of deity and became nothing. Sacrifice: it's a word that described the character of Jesus before He was ever born into this world. However we all know that His sacrifice didn't end there. In His death He paid the ultimate sacrifice for us all.

Read 1 John 2:2. Fill in the blanks below.

"He is the _____ for our sins, and not only ours but also for the sins of the _____".

In His death, Jesus paid the death penalty for our sins and reconciled us to God. His sacrifice made a way to turn aside God's divine wrath and cleanse us from our sin once and for all.

This atonement, also known as propitiation, can be traced all the way back to the Old Testament.

Read Exodus 25:17-22 and Leviticus 16:15-17.

What was the name of the cover that was placed on top of the ark of Testimony?

What took place above the cover between the two cherubim? (Exodus 25:22)

What was required in order to make atonement? Who made the atonement? Whom did the atonement sacrifice cover? Write down the details of the atonement sacrifice here. (Leviticus 16)

The Day of Atonement was the greatest day of the year for Israel. The Hebrew word for atone means "to cover." Old Testament sacrifices could not actually remove sins, only cover them. On this day, the people would confess their sins as a nation, and the high priest went into the Most Holy Place to make atonement for the nation's sins. Sacrifices were made and blood was shed so that the people's sin could be "covered" until Christ's sacrifice on the cross would give people the opportunity to have their sins removed forever.[9]

Read 1 John 4:10. What prompted God to send Jesus as our atoning sacrifice?

- ❏ **He was obligated to save us.**
- ❏ **He was motivated by His great love for us.**
- ❏ **He used the sacrifice as a way to manipulate His children into loving Him.**

As a mom, there's nothing more precious to me than checking in on my children and covering them for the night. I love to walk into each of their dimly lit rooms as they sleep and look upon their perfect, peaceful faces. In that quiet moment, it doesn't matter what kind of a day we've had or what words were spoken between the two of us. I am overcome with love. With great delight, I gently pull the covers up over their sweet little forms once more.

Now picture God covering His children. Just like a parent who carefully covers her child each night, God covers His children because of His great love for them. With tender care and a crazy, meticulous love, Father God pours the blood of Jesus out over our lives and covers us.

So, what's our response to this great sacrifice?

#1: OFFER A SACRIFICE OF PRAISE.

Read Psalm 107:22 and Hebrews 13:15.

According to Hebrews 13, how often are we to offer this sacrifice?

Through whom are we to offer up this sacrifice?

What's this sacrifice of praise called?

A worthy and right response for every believer in Christ is to offer the sacrifice of praise. Through Jesus, we're to lift our voices as an offering of thanks.

Sometimes praise comes easily. Like yesterday, right in the middle of winter, we had the most beautiful day. The sun was shining and temperatures rested in the low 70s. Because I'm not much of a winter-loving girl, I couldn't help but praise God for the spring-like heat of the sun that warmed my skin.

This verse, however, is talking about something different. It's talking about a continual – not conditional – act of praise.

When is it most difficult for you to praise the Lord?

Of course, we can and should praise God for every good and precious gift, but sacrifice doesn't happen when all is well and birds are chirping the hallelujah chorus. When tragedy comes – when all seems lost – when your circumstances leave you wanting – when you feel like you're in a pit of despair – each and every moment, regardless of our current situation, is an opportunity to praise. Thus, thanksgiving is the evidence of our acceptance of whatever He gives. It's our "yes" to Christ.

Did you notice in this verse that the sacrifice of praise is called the fruit of your lips? It's a fruit – not an act of service or a work. A work is an act of the flesh that is subject to the Law. A fruit is a product of cultivated hearts that stand in awe of God. It's something that grows naturally out of a heart that abides in Christ.[10]

Read John 15:8. Fill in the blanks.

It is to my Father's _____, that you _____ much _____, showing yourselves to be my _____.

Read Psalm 50:23. What does our sacrifice of praise mean to God?

When we live in gratitude we honor and glorify our Father. But, we also prepare the way for God to show us His salvation. Writer Ann Voskamp says, "Thanksgiving – giving thanks in everything – is what prepares the way for salvation's whole restoration. Our salvation in Christ is real, yet the completeness of that salvation is not fully realized in a life until the life realizes the need to give thanks."[11]

Describe a time in your life when you chose to praise the Lord in the midst of suffering? How did God redeem your dark season as you lifted Him up in praise?

#2: OFFER YOURSELF AS A LIVING SACRIFICE.

Read Romans 12:1.

I once heard a pastor say, "Every time you see the word 'therefore' in the Bible you should ask, 'what's it there for?'" To find out we need to read a few previous verses.

Please take a few minutes and read Romans 1:1 – 11:36 … No, not really! However, I will give you a quick recap.

Romans 1 through 11 describes in detail the compassion of God. It vividly portrays the sinfulness of all people, explaining how forgiveness is available through faith in Christ, and showing what believers experience in life through their new faith.

As a result of such mercy – in light of God's boundless grace and compassion - what are we to do? Our time. Our agenda. Our desires. Our energy. Daily – we must live in surrender. We are to be a living sacrifice, fully surrendered to God's will in our lives. Nothing less will do.

A.W. Tozer said, "Present your bodies… that is, present your vessel. A vessel that has not been presented will not be filled."[12] God cannot fill what He doesn't have.

This analogy of our bodies as a vessel resonates deep within me. Many times I've felt as if I were some type of container – desperately empty at times and other times unquestionably full.

What does it mean to present your vessel to God?

What type of vessel can be filled? Circle the correct answer.

An empty vessel   **A full vessel**

Empty hands lifted high to the God and Father of all grace and mercy … only empty vessels can be filled. Only the humble. Only those willing to sacrifice. Each day, we present our vessels: gloriously empty vessels waiting to be filled. Is it a sacrifice you are willing to make?

DAY 3
SUBMISSIVE

Ready to jump right in? How about a quick quiz first?

What are the first two actions of humility?

1.

2.

In order to find the third action attributed to the humble heart of Jesus, we'll start once again in Philippians 2.

> **"....taking the very nature of a servant, being made in human likeness; And being found in appearance as a man, he humbled himself and became obedient to death – even death on a cross!" Philippians 2:7-8**

The word for servant is actually better translated *bondservant* meaning, "A slave, one who gives himself up to another's will, devoted to another to the disregard of one's own interests." What a perfect description of Jesus: He made Himself nothing so that God could be all in and through Him. He was an empty vessel waiting to be filled by the Father.

In the book of John, Jesus spoke often of His relationship to the Father and His motive to live in full submission to Him.

Look up the following verses. Write down the ways that Jesus displayed a life marked by total dependence and submission to the Father.

John 5:19-20

John 5:30

John 6:38

John 7:16-18

John 8:28-29

These words tell us how it was that God was able to work His mighty redemptive will through Jesus. They show us the importance of the state of His heart in order to accomplish the Father's will. They give us a perfect picture of humility in action. Jesus lived to please the Father.

Even before He was sent to the cross, Jesus maintained His perfect posture of submission.

Read Matthew 26:36-45. As He agonized over what was to come, how did Jesus demonstrate His submissive spirit to the Father?

Jesus knew that for the first time in His life on Earth He would be totally separated from the Father and He could not even bear to think of it. Yet even in His agony He submitted perfectly.

This word, submission, is actually a military term meaning "to arrange [troop divisions] in a military fashion under the command of a leader." In non-military use, it is "to give over or yield to the power or authority of another." Can you see all of the ways that Jesus' life displayed this act of yielding, of deferring the power and authority of His Father? Each step He took, each word He spoke was perfectly dictated by the Father.

In one of my favorite passages of the Bible, John records the lesson taught by Jesus of the Vine and the branches.

Please read John 15:1-8. Answer the following questions.

What is the purpose of the vine?

What is the purpose of the branches?

What are the branches without the vine?

What does the story of the vine and branches teach us about humility and submission?

Jesus knew how a life of submission should be lived. He walked it every single day with His Father. Apart from the Father, Jesus did nothing! It is the way life was intended: man living in constant fellowship and perfect submission to the Father.

Read Romans 6:16 below from the New Living Translation.

"Don't you realize that you become the slave of whatever you choose to obey? You can be a slave to sin, which leads to death, or you can choose to obey God, which leads to righteous living."

The word slave used in this verse is the same word used in Philippians 2 to describe Jesus. It's someone who puts aside their own will in order to fulfill the will of another. It's someone who submits.

So, according to Romans 6:16, what is the evidence of our submission?

The root word of obedience in the New Testament gives a perfect word picture of submission. Broken down to its purest form, "to obey" means "to hear or listen under" or subordinate one's self to the person or thing heard. Our submission is manifested in ready obedience to the Lord.

Watching my children struggle and strain towards obedience has taught me so much in regards to my obedience to God. I have a friend who tells her kids that she wants them to obey "right away, all the way and in a happy way." Isn't that the same kind of obedience God requires of His children? No hesitation. No short cuts. No attitude. Just obey!

Is there some part of your life where you are having a difficult time "just obeying?" Why do you think you struggle to submit in this area?

Humility always places itself under God. It yields its will to the will of the Father. It says, "Yes" without reservation or hesitation.

We will close today with Charles Spurgeon's profound and thought provoking words about submission. "Submit yourselves unto God. Learn the sweetness of lying passive in His hand, and knowing no will but His: learn the blessedness of giving yourselves up entirely to His divine sway, for in so doing you will enter into heaven below."[13]

DAY 4
SERVANT'S HEART

The last action associated with humility is serving. Have you ever met someone who genuinely exhibited a heart to serve?

Many years ago, I met a man who single-handedly changed my perception of what it was to be a leader. He wasn't always in the front of the room but others followed him just the same. You see, everything about this guy exuded an "others first" mentality – this quiet act of servant hood that separated him from other men. This man – this servant leader – was always someone you could count on, someone you could trust and someone whom I just couldn't seem to get enough of. This man made me want to be a better woman. Watching him made me want to serve like him, like Jesus. Being loved by him changed me forever, so I married him.

Who do you know that exemplifies the quality of a servant's heart? Tell us a little about him or her.

Have you ever thought that the kingdom of God seems to have a backwards/upside down approach to living?

Read Matthew 20:26-28. According to this verse, what makes a person truly great?

"If you want to be first you must be last?" How counter-culture is that statement? We live in a world where if you are not first, you are fired. If you are not first, you will never be heard. If you are not first, you will not gain what is rightfully yours. If you are not first, you will most certainly be last. This last place finish will be void of success, lacking in value, and leave you feeling completely alone.

However, in God's Kingdom, the King of Kings and Lord of Lords makes Himself low. Those who are servants are the great ones. If you want to be first you must be last. Backwards and upside down, right?

Now read John 13:1-17.

I don't want you to miss three important points as we read undoubtedly the most common story used to convey the principle of serving.

#1: What Jesus knew …

According to verse 3, what did Jesus know?

What's the first word in verse 4? _____

Because of what Jesus knew in verse 3, He was able to do verse 4. How could He take on such a menial task? He knew who and whose He was.

How does knowing who you are in Christ give you confidence to serve others?

#2: What Jesus did…

According to verse 4–5, what did Jesus do for the disciples?

Matthew Henry explains how profound this act of service actually was. He describes how only the lowest ranking servants took on such a despicable act. He says, "… but for Christ to stoop to such a piece of drudgery as this may well excite our admiration."[14]

What did Jesus want to demonstrate by washing His disciples' feet? (Verse 1)

Jesus' heart to serve was motivated by His deep affection for those in His company, specifically those whom He had shared His life with and whom He had grown to love. His humility and great act of service began with His "family." The same is true for you and me. Where does our great act of service begin? It always begins at home.

How can we serve our family well as we go about the mundane tasks of our day to day? How can those same everyday tasks become sacred moments of serving our Savior? (See Colossians 3:23-24)

As a mom, I get to practice this "get up from the table" type of serving every day. Often before I take the first bite of my meal, someone is asking me to get up once again and serve. Have you experienced the same? I don't know about you, but watching Jesus' example to seize the opportunity to bless those in His care inspires me to push my chair back and tie on humility like an apron. It's our honor – to do like He did – and serve.

#3: When Jesus did it …

Read John 13:1 and Luke 22:14-15. According to these verses, when did this event take place; specifically what was about to happen to Jesus?

Jesus was fully disclosed to the events that were before Him. It was the night before His crucifixion. Can you imagine how Jesus might have felt that night?

What three words would you use to describe some of the emotions that Jesus might have experienced going into this Passover feast with His dearly loved followers?

Burdened. Distraught. Stressed. Yet He wasn't consumed with His impending doom. Instead, He turned His heart toward His brothers and served.

I can't help but reflect on my own life when I see the way Jesus entered into serving. Would I have seized the opportunity, like Jesus, even while my world was crumbling before me? Or am I only interested in serving when my schedule has cleared, when it's convenient or when I feel like it?

Can you think of a situation in which you chose to serve, even though it may not have seemed like the best timing, and you were able to participate in an extraordinary "God moment?"

So what's the result of extending this act of humility?

Read John 12:26 and John 13:17. Record your answer in the space provided.

Before we close for today, I want to get practical. As we have talked about before, clothing ourselves with Jesus has to be intentional. Merely reading about humility doesn't make us humble. Practicing humility is what changes us.

Next to each action of humility, write an action statement – something you can do in order to practice humility.

Selflessness:

Sacrifice:

Submission:

Service:

Each day is an opportunity for us to wrap ourselves in humility. As we keep our eyes on Jesus, selflessness, surrender, submission and service will begin to wardrobe our lives. Good work this week! Tomorrow we're going to talk about the opposition to humility: pride. Until then, practice, practice, practice!

DAY 5
PRIDE

Now here's a lesson I know a thing or two about. Pride.

In your own words, define the word pride.

What's the letter in the center of the word pride?

Oh yes. "I". Pretty much says it all, doesn't it? Pride is the sin of self. It's all consumed with me, myself and I. Pride thinks humility is weak. It tells the selfless – if you don't take care of No. 1, then who will. It tells the sacrificial – you better hold on to what you have or you'll wind up with nothing. It tells the submissive – the only person you can count on is yourself. It tells the servant – you are too busy with important things to waste your precious time on others.

While humility is embodied in Jesus, pride is embodied in someone else who is powerful too.

Read Ezekiel 28:12-17. Whom is it inferred that this verse is referring to?

The Fall Angel. The Father of lies. The Accuser. The Enemy. The Wicked One. Pride originated with Satan. Although the Bible doesn't give much information about him before his devastating fall, we can infer a few details about Satan – pre-fall – through these verses in Ezekiel.

According to these verses, what were some of Satan's strengths?

What was his position in the heavenlies?

What was the primary sin that caused Satan's fall?

Now read Isaiah 14:12-15. How many times does this verse use the word "I" to describe Satan?

Satan was blinded by the all-consuming "I". He wanted to exalt himself and make his name great. He was focused on his glory, his fame and his power. Not God's.

The Word is very clear about God's stance on pride.

What do Proverbs 16:5 and 16:18 warn will happen to the prideful?

In order to really understand how God feels about those who are prideful, we are going to look inside the lives of two powerful (and prideful) kings.

First, read Daniel 4:29-37. According to verse 30, whom was King Nebuchadnezzar bragging on?

What did God allow to happen to Nebuchadnezzar in order to humble him?

What caused his sanity to be restored and his honor and glory returned to him?

Now please read Acts 12:1-4, 21-23 – same sin, different outcome.

In order to please the Jewish officials and solidify his position among them, what was King Herod participating in?

What ultimately led to Herod's downfall?

Does it shock you to see the great lengths God will go to in order to humble His creation? Father God has been and will always be the only Holy of Holies. He's the only Great I Am. The only Sovereign One. He's the only one who deserves the glory, and His glory cannot be shared. It's for Him and Him alone. Nebuchadnezzar was willing to lift his eyes and humble himself before the Almighty, and God restored his life. The lesson went unlearned in the life of King Herod.

Read 1 Peter 5:5 and fill in the blanks.

All of you, _____ yourself in _____ toward one another, because God _____ the proud but gives _____ to the humble.

Clothing yourself with humility is a choice. It's a deliberate act. The word for "opposes" in this verse is a powerful word in Greek. It literally means, "To resist, to arrange in battle against." God is so serious about pride that He will allow His army to go to battle against the proud. Isn't that what we saw in the life of King Nebuchadnezzar and King Herod? Take heed: "those who walk in pride He is able to humble." (Daniel 4:37)

On the other end of the spectrum, what does God give to the humble?

When we're willing to clothe ourselves with humility, grace abounds. Grace, favor, the ability to deal with whatever comes our way. God says that His grace is sufficient for our every need. Humility has the ability to usher in such grace. What a promise!

When is it most difficult for you to humble yourself?

I've had many opportunities in my life to practice humility because pride is a pattern I've grown accustomed to. I honestly didn't know how I could serve or encourage or council without making it about me. I certainly didn't know how to use the gifts God has given me without wanting (or needing) a little pat on the back. As a result, I've experienced the remorse of my sin and the pain of being humbled.

However, along the way God has graced me with new eyes to see my pride for what it is. Because of His compassion and kindness, I've been given the strength to bend my knees and lay down humbly before Him – to surrender and sacrifice my sin of self. Although I'm sure I'll have the opportunity to practice humility time and time again, I'm beginning to learn how to walk with my eyes fixed upward on Him and not on the all-consuming "I".

Ever experienced the humbling hand of the Father? If so, tell us a little about it.

How can this promise of grace encourage you to choose the higher road of humility each time?

"He who humbles himself will be exalted" (Luke 14:11). Humility is rewarded and is worth the choice each and every time. It was the way of Jesus. Let's be imitators of our Lord and Savior and gird ourselves.

CHAPTER 5

GENTLENESS AND PATIENCE

DAY 1
GENTLENESS

We've made it to the end of the first verse in our primary text. Let's see how well you can remember what we've learned.

> **Pop Quiz: Write out Colossians 3:12 by memory. Underline the last two virtues in the verse. (If you have to peek that's OK, too. It's the exercise of writing it that counts.)**

> **What are the next two virtues that we are instructed to put on, according to Colossians 3:12?**

Both of these virtues are part of the fruit of the Spirit (Galatians 5:22-23). This fruit is the spontaneous work of the Holy Spirit inside of us when we are born again. It describes the character traits of Jesus, and when fully submitted to Him, they're the fruit of our lives as well.

The first virtue we will consider this week, *gentleness*, is a descriptive word in the Bible that I've regretfully skimmed over. For some reason, the word blends into the page as if it isn't even there. Perhaps if it were clothing, it would look like camouflage. But what's behind this word? Is there something hidden behind its soft exterior?

Before we begin, what are your thoughts about the character trait of gentleness? Do you skim over the word like I have or does it resonate in some way with you?

Prautes, or gentleness, is defined as, "mild, gentle in spirit, meek." The word meek gives great insight into the meaning of gentleness. Meekness is often misunderstood for weakness but it's actually quite the opposite. Meekness is a quiet strength – a controlled strength – it's a strength that accommodates another's weaknesses. Picture a soothing wind blowing across your cheeks. That same wind has the potential to become a powerful storm; it is power under control.

Today we'll look into the lives of two men described as meek: Jesus and Moses.

Read the following verses. Write down how each man is depicted.

Matthew 11:29

Numbers 12:3

These two certainly possessed this beautiful quality of controlled strength.

Read Matthew 26:47-54. How does Jesus display gentleness in the Garden of Gethsemane when He was arrested?

Sadly, I'm more like Peter, sword blazing, ready to take off an ear or two in the heat of battle. However, Jesus responded differently than Peter. Onlookers might have thought: What is He doing? Isn't He going to stand up for Himself? What kind of leader is He? Why is He being so weak?

Little did they know that Jesus was showing amazing strength in His power of restraint. After all, He had a massive army at His disposal (specifically 12 legions of angels which amounts to tens of thousands of angles), but He restrained His use of power because He knew what He had to do. He put aside His strength and power as a king and in meekness (not weakness) exemplified a king who would do anything for His people. He's not a domineering tyrant, but a meek, gentle and loving King.

Gentleness has the ability to bear criticism and hostility without bitterness or resentment. It stems from a complete trust in God. Don't you find it fascinating that Jesus navigated through life with unwavering faith in God's will? He had no need to defend Himself, fight for His rights or retaliate because He believed fully in God's sovereignty and goodness.

Can you see how gentleness is so perfectly woven together with humility? Because Jesus had fully submitted to the power of His Father, He had no need to claim power of His own.

Now let's look at Moses – labeled as the meekest man on the face of the Earth.

Read Numbers 12:1-15. What were Miriam and Aaron complaining about?

Which of the following statements best summarizes Moses' defense? Check all that apply.

❑ **Moses defended himself by using his leadership and authority over them.**
❑ **Moses said nothing to defend himself.**
❑ **God defended Moses by asserting His leadership and authority.**
❑ **No defense was given. Their complaints were valid.**

Moses could have stood up for himself and showed Miriam and Aaron who was boss. But he didn't. He made no effort to defend himself or retaliate. He even begged God to take away Miriam's punishment of leprosy after God came to his aid. Moses had yielded to God and had no desire to justify his own renown. However, you can be sure Moses would always stand up to defend the name of his Most Holy Father.

Psalm 37 gives us a perfect portrait for the meek.

Read Psalm 37:3-11.

Notice the four characteristics that David lists as strengths of the meek.

1. **The meek trust in God.** (Verse 3)
Both Jesus and Moses believed God. They believed He was who He said He was, and they believed that He could do what He said He would do. They trusted in Him. The word trust is a picture of leaning in on someone with full confidence in their ability to hold you up. That is how Jesus and Moses lived: fully leaning into the sovereign will of the Father.

2. **The meek commit their ways to the Lord.** (Verse 5)
Because they trust in Him, those that are meek are able to confidently place their burdens in the hands of the Father. In Hebrew this verse is translated "roll your way upon the Lord." The meek *roll* each burden, each dream, each care of their load onto the Lord.

Read Psalm 55:22. What promise does this verse give to those that cast their cares on the Lord?

We often say that we trust God, yet the piles of burdens we carry each day tell differently. Do you trust that the same strength that sustains you is also able to carry your burdens?

Can you think of any burdens today that you may need to *roll* to the Lord? If so, list them here.

3. **The meek are still before the Lord and wait patiently for Him.** (Verse 7)
With their load safely tucked away with Father God, the meek now have the ability to be quiet before the Lord and wait. They have a kind of steady calm that comes from knowing that God is in control. They know that He is gracious and will work things out for the best. Meek people have a quiet steadiness about their lives in the midst of upheaval.

One of my favorite verses in the Bible is Psalm 46:10.

"Be still, and know that I am God; I will be exalted among the nations, I will be exalted in the earth."

Be still. Relax. Let go. Stop your striving. Be quiet and recognize that I am God. That's what the meek do. While sitting in the presence of the Lord with quiet reverence, the meek confidently wait on the one and only One with authority and power. They truly understand that power is at work, and it does not come from them.

4. **The meek don't worry and remain calm**. (Verse 7b-8)
Can you see the ways that these four characteristics of the meek compound together? They trust. They commit their ways. They are still and wait. Lastly, they don't fret or become anxious in the waiting. They don't get caught up or riled up in what's going on around them. They show a controlled strength that's able to remain at ease.

According to Psalm 37:11, what are the rewards of the meek?

1.

2.

Worthy rewards? Yes! Once again the English translation of this Hebrew text only waters down the significance of these words. What is God's promise to the meek?

#1: They will step into their full inheritance in this life.
The meek will experience the contentment of their "pleasant places" expressed through the mouth of David in Psalm 16.

> **"Lord, you have assigned me my portion and my cup; you have made my lot secure. The boundary lines have fallen for me in pleasant places; surely I have a delightful inheritance." Psalm 16:5-6**

#2: They will experience an abundance of peace – unlimited peace – a peace without measure.
Before you go on thinking that this peace is just "a state of tranquility" (which is enough already); take a moment to read all that this Hebrew word encompasses. *Shalom* means, "Completeness, soundness, welfare, safety, health, prosperity, and contentment, friendship of human relationships and with God, especially in covenant relationship." That's the "full meal deal" of peace, wouldn't you agree?

Truly – blessed are the meek!

DAY 2
A QUIET AND GENTLE SPIRIT

Today we'll be looking at another aspect of gentleness that pertains specifically to women.

Read 1 Peter 3:3-4.

What kind of beauty should women focus on?

☐ **Ageless beauty**
☐ **The perfect wardrobe**
☐ **Inner beauty**
☐ **No beauty – it's all vanity**

Specifically, what kind of "looks" is God most attracted to?

After learning a little bit more about gentleness yesterday, what do you think it means to have a quiet and gentle spirit?

Truth be told, I've struggled with the concept of a "quiet and gentle spirit" because it challenged my perception of being a strong woman. I've prided myself in being strong and knew that my personality wasn't quiet or gentle. Without saying it out loud, those who are tender came across as weak. However, as I've come to know Jesus, as I've studied His character and watched Him move about in a gracious and gentle way, I've learned differently. My strong façade must crumble if I truly want to be like Him – if I want to put on the wardrobe of Christ.

Read 1 Peter 3:4 again, this time in the Amplified version.

"But let it be the inward adorning and beauty of the hidden person of the heart, with the incorruptible and unfading charm of a gentle and peaceful spirit, which [is not anxious or wrought up, but] is very precious in the sight of God." 1 Peter 3:4 AMP

The first thing I had to learn about a *quiet and gentle spirit* is that this isn't talking about my personality. The verse doesn't say "a quiet and gentle personality," but a quiet and gentle *spirit*. The "inner self" – the "hidden person" – these words describe who we are deep in our souls.

The word quiet actually means "tranquil and peaceful." It describes a person who is secure, peaceful and at rest from the inside out. (Did you just take a huge sigh of relief too?) I know this may sound absurd, but I'm thrilled that this quietness is about my soul and not my mouth!

In Isaiah 30:15 we're told that when we're able to find this quietness of the soul, we find strength. There's confidence and power in a quiet soul, in a soul that's at peace. The temptation, however, is to believe the exact opposite is true. So we hang on to worry and anxiety, we hang on to the noise, and we desperately reach for the reins of control. Unknowingly, we believe the lie that our strength rests in our ability to keep it all together, and our souls are dominated by anything but quiet. Can you relate?

But God...

Two of my favorite words when linked together.

But God offers a better way. He offers peace. He only asks that we be willing to follow Him - to stop long enough to lie down in the green pastures that He provides - to linger for a moment along the edge of His quiet waters. It is in those sacred places that our souls are restored (Psalm 23:2-3). It is there, with Him, that we find rest.

I want to give you one more picture before we move on.

Read Zephaniah 3:17. Fill in the blanks.

He will take great delight in you, he will _____ you with His _____, he will rejoice over you with singing.

Can you picture it? Even if it's a stretch for you, please try to imagine this scene as though it were playing life sized on a movie screen. Imagine the beauty, the majesty, the tenderness of the Father loving on His child in the most extravagant of ways. Imagine Him dancing over you! Imagine His glory shining down on your little frame! Imagine the outpouring of His love - a love that quiets you to the depths of your soul - a love that gives you peace. That's what God is after!

Take a moment to think about the state of your soul. Is your spirit at rest? Spend whatever time necessary to talk to the Father about your soul's need for peace.

OK – back to work we go....

Women described as having a quiet and gentle spirit are:

1. TEACHABLE

Read James 1:19-21.

In order to understand this passage in context, we need to start at the end and work backwards.

Referring to verse 21, fill in the blanks below.

Therefore, get rid of all moral filth and evil that is so prevalent and _____ _____ the word planted in you, which can save you.

The words "humbly accept" is also translated "in meekness or with a gentle spirit." Only the gentle in spirit have soil that's ready to receive the seed of the Word of Truth.

Below are characteristics that enable these hearts to be fertile and receptive to teaching:

- **THEY ARE *QUICK TO LISTEN*.**

Are you eager to take in the Word of God? Do you offer a willing ear to hear the voice of God? Those who are "quick to listen" prioritize their time in God's Word and position themselves to humbly receive, but who is responsible for opening their ears?

Read Isaiah 50:4-5. Reflect on your answer here.

- **THEY ARE *SLOW TO SPEAK*.**

It's difficult to listen when you're talking all of the time. Those with a quiet and gentle spirit are careful to use their power of restraint to keep their mouths closed. When they do open their mouths, they are cautious with their words.

Read Proverbs 10:19 and 17:27. Note what they teach about restraining your words.

Sometimes it's not our mouths that hinder us from listening. Often, it's our thoughts that become our biggest distraction. Have you ever caught yourself thinking about what you want to say (rehearsing your speech) rather than actually listening to what others are saying? It takes a disciplined mind to turn off its "speech" in order to truly listen.

- **THEY ARE *SLOW TO BECOME ANGRY.***

In context, "slow to become angry" refers to how you respond to God or the Word of God.

Read Proverbs 14:29. Explain why you think some become angry when they hear God's Word.

Quick to listen, slow to speak and slow to become angry: these are the characteristics of hearts receptive to teaching – hearts that are pliable and moldable in the hands of the Father.

2. WISE

Read James 3:13 written below.

"Who among you is wise and understanding? Let him show by his good behavior his deeds in the gentleness of wisdom." (NASB)

Now read James 3:17-18 from The Message.

"Real wisdom, God's wisdom, begins with a holy life and is characterized by getting along with others. It is gentle and reasonable, overflowing with mercy and blessings, not hot one day and cold the next, not two-faced. You can develop a healthy, robust community that lives right with God and enjoy its results only if you do the hard work of getting along with each other, treating each other with dignity and honor."

In both of these verses, wisdom is described as *gentle*. Matthew Henry says, "When we are mild and calm, we are best able to hear reason, and best able to speak it. Wisdom produces meekness and meekness increases wisdom … Wisdom is gentle: not being rude or overbearing in conversation, nor harsh or cruel in temper. Therefore, someone with a quiet and gentle spirit is composed and under control. They don't lash out in anger."[15]

Read Proverbs 15:1. How does this verse relate to "the gentleness of wisdom"?

So when you combine the serenity of the quiet to the restrained power of the gentle, what do you get? You get someone you want to be around and someone you want to be!

Don't you find it pretty amazing that God speaks only to women about the virtuous trait of a quiet and gentle spirit? Why is that?

Think about this….

A woman with a quiet and gentle spirit knows who she is in Christ. She's confident in God's measureless love for her and secure in walking along side Jesus each day. She is calm – not combative – and deals gently with everyone she comes in contact with. Like the rising of the sun, she is strong and steady, careful not to explode like fireworks with each dilemma of the day. She carries herself with dignity and doesn't hide behind outrageous attire to draw people her way. This woman exudes confidence in her role as a woman (and all that comes with that) and the way the Lord has uniquely gifted her to carry out His purpose each day. She has nothing to prove, nothing to demand and no other agenda to push. She is at peace in Christ.

God knows the strength of a woman. He knows what power she holds when fully submitted to Him. In the words of Paul, by the grace of God "Let your gentleness be evident to all. The Lord is near." (Philippians 4:5)

DAY 3
PATIENCE – ENDURING OTHERS

I trudge into today dragging my feet. Most virtues I'm eager to learn about and excited to put into practice. But patience? Don't get me wrong: I want and desperately need this type of fortitude. However, I've had some experience with this admirable trait and know from experience that it isn't something you miraculously stumble upon. This trait – the precious virtue of patience – must be practiced. Over and over and over again.

The very last virtue in Colossians 3:12 that we are told to put on is patience, or *makrothumia* in Greek. *Makrothumia* is defined as, "endurance, constancy, steadfastness, perseverance, longsuffering, slowness in avenging wrongs." The Amplified version defines *patience* as "tireless and long-suffering, and has the power to endure whatever comes with good temper". Those who exhibit patience are said to have a long fuse. They can burn and burn without ever blowing up.

Our patience, or lack of patience, is tested in two different ways: through our interactions with other people and in enduring difficult circumstances. We'll spend our time today on the first: enduring others.

> **Read 1 Timothy 1:15-16. What did Paul say Jesus had to exercise in dealing with him, the self-proclaimed "worst of sinners"?**

Let's go back and review what kind of man Paul was before his conversion.

> **Read Acts 8:1-3 and 9:1-2. Write down three facts about Saul, Paul's name pre-conversion.**
>
> 1.
>
> 2.
>
> 3.

Jesus showed unlimited patience to Paul in order to bring him to the point of his miraculous conversion. He shows the same patience to us too.

> **Fill in the blanks as you read 2 Peter 3:15:**
>
> **Bear in mind that our Lord's _____ means _____, just as our dear Paul also wrote you with the wisdom that God gave him.**

"Patience means salvation"? The NET Version words this verse as, "Regard the patience of our Lord as salvation…"

How has Christ shown patience with you? What things in your life did Jesus have to patiently endure watching before you came to the knowledge of His saving grace?

Thankfully, God deals ever so patiently with us. In the Old Testament, the Bible uses the term "slow to anger" to describe this same quality of patience.

Look up the following verses. Write down the circumstances in which God shows patience toward His beloved children.

Exodus 34:5-7

Nehemiah 9:16-18

Psalm 103:8-10

Because God is patient with us, we should show the same courtesy to others. The kind of patience God asks of us is not grit-your-teeth endurance, yet that's the only kind of patience you and I can muster in our own strength. It's only by the Holy Spirit that we can exercise the supernatural ability to endure others. By faith, we must put it on.

Think about the people in your life that cause the most friction – those better known as "holy sandpaper". Without naming names, in what ways do those kinds of people rub you the wrong way?

Check the box that applies to the "holy sandpaper" people in your life.

- ☐ **Sign me up for a few more friends like that.**
- ☐ **I welcome any and every opportunity to love on them.**
- ☐ **They bring out nothing but the best in me.**
- ☐ **None of the above.**

Did you answer "none of the above"? Me too! Isn't it amazing how we allow these trying people in our lives to push us to our limits so quickly that we often don't know what happened to us? And there we are – with all our ugliness hanging out! I'm beginning to realize that those very people have been put in my life for a grand purpose: to expose my ugliness. The question is: What do I do with it once it's been exposed? God's desire is for you and me to deal with that which has been exposed. He wants us to grow and He uses the people around us, especially those who expose us for who we really are, to bring about that change.

How can changing your perspective about difficult people help you to respond more patiently with them?

Read 1 Corinthians 13:4. Love is _____...

How many of you know this verse by heart but still looked it up just to make sure you *really* had to write down that word? Patient. Yes, that's what it says. Love is patient. Really? Why does love have to be patient first? If you have kids, does love really still have to maintain its defined biblical order? Because I l-o-v-e my children but patient would not always describe my love for them. Without question my children are absolute professionals at testing my patience. Yet sadly, my three offspring, the ones I love to pieces, expose me.

The recipe for a blow out – a mommy meltdown, if you will – is usually the same. I have an agenda. I've planned and managed poorly. I'm running late (and I really dislike being late). For some reason, the kids are not privy to my so-called emergency. Because kids, if you haven't noticed, take life as it comes. They're fully in the moment; perfect little experts of the "now". And mommy – well, this mommy is off to the races and moving too fast to get slowed by every little "now" moment. So it happens: boom! My temper explodes. There I am with all of my ugliness exposed and dripping all over the faces of my little ones.

Or I could choose to respond a different way; one that I'm trying to practice more often. When I feel the fuse shortening and my anger starting to boil, I can stop. Breathe. And submit to Jesus. After all, Jesus is patient and He promises to "meet all of my needs according to His glorious riches" (Philippians 4:19). So, Jesus can be my patience. He can be the answer to my "now" moment.

Instead of blaming my three little works in progress for not being complete, perfect works of art, I can recognized that I too am a "work in progress", and that he who began a good work in (me) will carry it on to completion until the day of Christ Jesus. (Philippians 1:6)

DAY 4
PATIENCE – ENDURING LIFE

Yesterday we talked about the difficulty in enduring others. Today we're going to rest on another aspect of patience. Often times, it's the circumstances in our lives (not the people) that require a heavy dose of patience. I don't have to tell you that life doesn't always work out like we want it to, and seldom does life happen according to our timetable.

God asks us to wait. WAIT – that's one four letter word that has a way of torturing me. I like the word NOW much better. Instant gratification makes me happy. Thankfully, however, God is much more interested in my character than my happiness. He wants me to become more like Jesus and He's willing to cause delay in my life if it will bring me closer to Him.

Let's look to David, one of our Old Testament heroes, as he waited on God. It seems as though David was a professional at waiting. After all, fifteen years passed between the moment he was anointed king to the day he wore the crown.

Read Psalm 40:1-3. What can we infer that David was doing as he waited on God, according to verse 1?

While David waited patiently on God to save him, he prayed.

What do you tend to do most often when you are waiting on circumstances to change or come about in your life?

I do many things when I'm waiting on God for circumstances to change. Sure, I pray. I also pout, complain, grumble and worry. I'm not exactly the poster child for abounding in patience. David did much better than I. He diligently sought the Lord as he waited patiently.

I love what happens next. We're never told that God answered David's prayer just like he was hoping. It actually doesn't tell us that He gave him an answer at all. Instead, God does three things for David (and for us – for that matter) when we cry out to Him.

1. God *really* hears us when we cry out to Him.

Verse one says that God "turned to me and heard my cry". Other translations say, "He inclined to me and heard my cry". What a beautiful picture of our loving God: bending down from His heavenly throne because He heard the cry of one of His own. When we cry out to our Heavenly Father, God not only hears us but He stoops down to hear each cry of our heart. Not one word uttered from your lips will ever fall to the ground without first going through the filter of our Lord and Savior.

Do you find any comfort in knowing that the God of the Universe hears each and every word you cry out to Him in those times of wait? What does this truth mean to you?

2. God gives peace.

God does better than give us what we ask. Instead He gives us what we need so that we might endure through our circumstance in order to bring about growth in our lives.

What does verse two say God does for David?

Have you ever in a season of wait fallen into a pit of despair? Has it ever felt like "miry clay"? I definitely know the feeling of slippery mud under my feet. In my impatience I've sunk into a pit of depression, eyes focused only on the dreaded unknown, with no foothold in sight. In desperation I've cried out to God and He's given me this same foothold: a miraculous boost to solid ground. When I'm no longer slipping, peace abounds – a peace beyond all understanding.

Can you describe a time in your life when God answered your cry to Him by giving you the indescribable gift of peace instead of the answer you thought you were longing for?

3. God gives joy.

Upon encountering God in his time of need, David received the gift of joy from his Father. "He put a new song in my mouth, a hymn of praise to our God." (Psalm 40:3) Joy comes from experiencing Jesus, not from getting our wish list met. We're given unexplainable joy despite our circumstances, and with it the supernatural ability to continue to endure to the end.

Remember that four letter word I really dislike: wait. After a little studying, I think I might have to change my mind. Are you ready for this? According to the Hebrew definition, wait means "look for, hope, expect, to bind together by twisting." What? "To bind together by twisting"?

In order to get a picture of this definition in action, read the following verses. Each time you see the word "wait", insert in its place "bind together by twisting". What else does God promise to those who wait on Him?

Isaiah 40:31

Isaiah 64:4

Lamentations 3:24-26

How does this new found definition change how you view waiting?

Perseverance is another aspect of patiently enduring or sustaining hardships.

Read James 1:2-4. When we hang in there, twist ourselves together with Jesus and stay under the hardship, what is the promised outcome?

Not only do we walk away having grown from the circumstance, but what else does James say is the result of persevering in a trial according to James 1:12?

Now read Romans 5:3-5. Trace the progression of growth listed in these verses as you fill in the blanks.

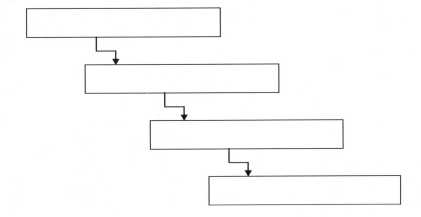

Only our sovereign and loving Father can transform suffering into hope. With hope, we have the boldness we need to once again endure with confidence.

Are you in a season of wait? If so, tell us a little bit about it. What are you holding out in hope for?

I want to end today with a verse that has encouraged me in my seasons of wait.

I am still confident of this: I will see the goodness of the Lord in the land of the living. Wait for the Lord; be strong and take heart and wait for the Lord. Psalm 27:13-14

Let this verse be your battle cry. You *will* see the goodness of the Lord…so stand firm. Twist up and wait on Him! He is certainly worth the waiting.

DAY 5
A POWERFUL COMBINATION

Today we'll start with some reflection. I'm not always mindful of stopping and absorbing what I just studied and learned. Sometimes the pursuit of more (more knowledge, more inspiration, more of His presence) drives me forward before my heart has had time to catch up.

Today I'm forcing us to stop in front of the dressing mirror to reflect for a moment.

Tell me what you have learned or been reminded of as we studied gentleness? Did its camouflage-like appearance fool you into underestimating the strength of this virtue?

What about patience? In what ways are you challenged as you wait?

Which type of patience do you currently have to practice: enduring life, enduring others or both?

Before we close for the week, I want to spend some time talking about how these two powerful characteristics come together in perfect unity through the life of Jesus.

Our main text is Matthew 12:15-21, which records the fulfillment of a prophecy originally recorded in Isaiah 42:1-4. Take a moment to read both. Write Matthew 12:20 in the space provided.

In one powerful prophecy, we are given a glimpse into what would be later fulfilled as the gentleness of Jesus. In the verse you just wrote out above, two common objects are used as illustrations for the different types of people Jesus is passionate about pursuing with gentleness and patience.

A BRUISED REED

According to commentary, a reed is a tall, hollow-stemmed plant that grows along river beds. Reeds were used as symbols of *weakness* and *fickleness* in the Bible. When the Roman soldiers mocked Jesus in Matthew 27:29, they placed a reed in His right hand to let everyone know that they thought He was powerless.[16]

The English translation of bruised doesn't convey the complexity of the word in Greek. This word, *suntemo*, means "break, to break in pieces, shiver, to tread down, to break down, crush, to tear one's body and shatter one's strength."

Therefore, a bruised reed can be used to describe people who are:

1. Crushed, broken and discouraged
2. Full of doubt or fear
3. Weak and oppressed

Read the following verse. Underline how our gentle and patient Savior tends to these bruised reeds.

"The Spirit of the Lord God is upon me, because the Lord has anointed and qualified me to preach the Gospel of good tidings to the meek, the poor and afflicted; He has sent me to bind up and heal the brokenhearted, to proclaim liberty to the [physical and spiritual] captives and the opening of the prison and of the eyes to those who are bound." Isaiah 61:1, Amplified

Jesus heals. He stays close. He holds up. He strengthens. He never breaks us or deserts us or gets tired of our need for Him. Our frailty doesn't scare Him away, and our brokenness will never render us useless.

Actually it's the opposite.

In 2 Corinthians, Paul says he prayed three times for his "thorn" to be taken away from him. Although we don't know what Paul's "thorn" was, we know that he considered it his weakness. God answered him in by saying, "My grace is sufficient for you, for my power is made perfect in weakness." The verse goes on to say (Paul speaking), "Therefore I will boast all the more gladly about my weaknesses, so that Christ's power may rest on me. That is why, for Christ's sake, I delight in weaknesses, in insults, in hardships, in persecutions, in difficulties. For when I am weak, then I am strong." (2 Corinthians 12:9-10.)

When is Jesus' power "made perfect"?

When are we truly at our strongest? Why?

Now read 1 Corinthians 1:26-31. Check each box that describes the type of person that Jesus came to save:

❑ **Foolish**
❑ **Wise**
❑ **Lowly**
❑ **Weak**
❑ **Strong**

Here we go again: backwards and upside down. According to verses 29-31, why does Jesus choose these types of people?

A SMOLDERING WICK

The second analogy used is that of a smoldering wick. Again, according to commentary, wicks were made out of linen. When the oil ran out the flame would flicker and emit a cloud of smelly smoke. All the dirt that was around the flame would start smoking as well. The smoke would become an irritant so people would just reach out and snuff it out.[17]

People seen as a smoldering wick might be those who are:

1. Dim or faint in faith
2. Burned out and hopeless
3. Offensive

My children love to blow out candles. My youngest has been known to get dangerously close to a flame just for the thrill of blowing it out. Sometimes as a treat I light five tea lights on our kitchen table for a little dinner mood lighting. The premise is that if the kids eat all of their food, when we are all finished they can each blow out a candle. Surprisingly, it works. They all scarf down what's on their plates just to have their chance at putting out the glowing flame.

Jesus, however, isn't in the business of blowing out candles. He takes no delight in snuffing out a flame. Even when we are barely lit, He takes great care to tend to our flame.

Read Psalm 18:28. Who does the Psalmist say keeps his lamp burning?

The concept of a fire or flame is used throughout both the Old and New Testament. From cover to cover, a fire is used to describe or contain the presence of God. In Exodus 3, God spoke to Moses through a burning bush. As the Israelites wandered through the desert, a pillar of fire followed them at night and gave them warmth and light. When the law was given to Moses in the form of the Ten Commandments, "Mount Sinai was covered with smoke, because the Lord descended on it in fire" (Exodus 19:18). Lastly, when the Holy Spirit was poured out over the crowd of new believers on the day of Pentecost, tongues of fire rested on each one of them. God truly is a consuming fire! (Hebrews 12:29)

Just as the small fire of a burning candle draws my kids towards its flame, the fire of God also draws us near. It is inviting and appealing, with a radiating heat that warms our heart and comforts our soul. When we choose the flame and receive the fire, we too radiate with the fire of God. It's Christ in us that draw people near, providing comfort and warmth to all of those lost in the dark.

A bruised reed and a smoldering wick … both are safe in the hands of our gentle and patient Savior. Can the same be said of you?

CHAPTER 6

FORGIVENESS AND LOVE

Time for a little closet check: How's your wardrobe looking? The closet of Jesus is a pretty impressive sight – one worth pursing with all our might, wouldn't you agree? Jesus is worth every ounce of our attention and more. As my pastor always says, "Jesus is way better than we think He is!"

Which of the virtues we've studied so far are the most difficult for you to put on?

- ❑ **Compassion**
- ❑ **Kindness**
- ❑ **Humility**
- ❑ **Gentleness**
- ❑ **Patience**
- ❑ **All of them – UGH!**

I hope you have found great comfort in knowing that you don't have to toil and spin to achieve any of these virtues for God. The list above adds only one thing to our daily to do list: we must choose to put them on. Clothing ourselves with Jesus is a choice we have the privilege of making each day. We choose His grace over our works, His compassion for our insensitivity, His kindness for our spite, His humility for our pride, His gentleness for our abrasiveness, and His patience for our huge lack thereof. You see – these traits are only ours through Him who lives in us. I don't know about you, but that's a huge sigh of relief for me. I'm quite sure I am nothing without Him!

DAY 1
RECEIVING FORGIVENESS

Let's press on. Please write Colossians 3:13.

It's no coincidence that forgiveness is listed towards the end of this long list of virtues. If we don't have the heart of compassion and the hand of kindness, if we continue without an attitude of humility or a gentle and patient spirit, how do we even consider "bearing" with our neighbors?

"To bear" with each other is a present tense word that is better translated, "to endure, put up with, tolerate." We're commanded to continuously endure each other. Does that make you smile even a little bit? It does me. God knows that some of us are flat out difficult to deal with. In the spirit of preserving unity within the body and some sanity among each other, we have to learn to make allowances for other's faults.

What does it mean to you to "make allowances for each other's faults"? Give some examples of the faults you continue to endure (without naming names, of course).

Paul then takes us a step further and commands us to forgive. Whereas bearing with each other relates to our present, forgiving relates to our past. He says, "Forgive whatever grievances you may have against one another. Forgive as the Lord forgave you" (Colossians 3:13). In order to understand how we are to forgive, we need to first understand how the Lord forgives us.

Read John 8:1-11.

Picture the scene. Jesus is sitting amongst a crowd of people teaching when in walks the teachers of the law and Pharisees, dragging behind them an "adulterous" woman. Using this poor woman as a pawn, they stand her before the group, humiliated, challenging Jesus on what they are to do with her. If He is lax and tells them to let her go, then they would accuse Him of not abiding by Moses' law (which says that both man and woman are to be stoned). However, if He holds a strict line and tells them to stone her, He would be in trouble with the Romans who forbid that Jews carry out their own executions.

Instead of falling into their trap, what does Jesus do?

There have been many speculations as to what He was writing but one thing we can be sure of: God the Father prompted it. Jesus was so well versed in the Word of God that He might have used the moment to write down some scripture.

Look up Jeremiah 17:13. How does this scripture reference names "written in the dust"?

Writing the names of the accusers in the sand would have spoken volumes to these 'Bible Scholars' for they certainly would have known whom this verse was referring to.

Jesus then calls for the man without sin to cast the first stone, and one by one they walk away, eldest to youngest. When confronted with their own sin before God, the stones fell to the ground. Only Jesus remains – the sinless one – still bent over next to the woman writing in the sand.

Why do you think the eldest in the crowd were the first to leave?

Look again at the brief conversation between the woman and Jesus in verses 10 and 11 and fill in the blanks.

"Then neither do I _____ you.' Jesus declares. 'Go now and _____ your life of _____.'"

Jesus doesn't condemn the woman. Instead He grants her a pardon and calls her to a new life apart from sin.

Can you picture yourself in our story? Who would you have been: one of the accusers or the one who pardons? Think about it this way: do you spend more of your time judging and condemning others, or do you take advantage of each opportunity to readily forgive?

Jesus forgives. Immediately. Completely. Unconditionally. He forgives. To forgive means, "to cease to feel resentment for, to pardon." Pardoning is the act of excusing an offense without requiring a penalty.

Look up the following verses and note how God the Father pardons the sins of His children. Put a star next to the verse that speaks the most to you.

Psalm 103:12

Isaiah 38:17

Isaiah 43:25

Isaiah 44:22

Micah 7:19

I would've marked Isaiah 43:25. It reads, "I, even I, am he who blots out your transgressions, for my own sake, and remembers your sins no more." The word for "blots out" is the Hebrew word *machah,* which means, "To wipe out, obliterate, to blot out." Can you guess where else this word is used in the Old Testament? Did your mind wander back to Noah and the flood?

The forgiveness of God is like the mighty floodwaters that raised up to wash away all that was evil and unclean during the days of Noah. Although God promises to never again wipe out the whole Earth by flood, He still continues to wipe out *and* wash away our sins. Forgive and forget is the motto God lives by.

The problem many have isn't in God's ability to forgive but in their ability to accept and receive it. How do we fully take hold of such boundless mercy?

The text I'm going to take you to now may seem like a rabbit trail, but you'll understand shortly why we're here.

Read Romans 4:13-22. Fill in the blanks. (In order to really process Paul's teaching here, you may want to read the text a few times. Once was not enough for me!)

Verse 13: "It was not though the law that Abraham and his offspring received the promise...but through the righteousness that comes _____."

Verse   16:   "Therefore,   the   promise   comes _____ _____ ..."

Abraham received the full bounty of the promise of God *by faith.* He believed and was fully persuaded that God had the power to do what He had promised.

Now, watch as Paul perfectly applies this text about the faith of Abraham to our study on forgiveness.

Pick right back up where you left off – in Romans 4:23-25. How are we, like Abraham, credited to Him as righteousness? In other words, how do we gain a right standing before God?

How do we fully accept and receive the forgiveness of God? By faith! We believe that God has the power to do what He's promised. And we let ourselves be forgiven …

Because you know as well as I do that sometimes we hold the biggest grudges on ourselves. We just can't seem to let ourselves be forgiven. The guilt is too great. Sadly, it's as if we take a look at the power and redemptive work of Jesus on the cross and say, "Thanks for being willing to take the scorn and shame of my sin but I'd like to hold on to that, if you don't mind."

David didn't take for granted the forgiveness of God, and not because he was a man without sin. A quick look into Biblical history would tell you that although he grieved deeply over his sins (like adultery, murder and lies), he fully believed in the power of God's forgiveness.

Flip back a little and read Romans 4:6-8. Whom does David call blessed?

David praises those who have been forgiven – those who rely completely on the grace of God to cover their sins. He cheers on our faith and rallies us on to experience the joy of forgiveness.

If you haven't received the full bounty of God's forgiveness, today is the day to boldly step before the throne of God and receive His mercy. Confess and believe that God is faithful and just and will forgive your sins and purify you from all unrighteousness. (1 John 1:9)

DAY 2
EXTENDING FORGIVENESS

Yesterday we began by wrapping our minds around the concept of the forgiveness of God. Today we're going to talk about what forgiveness looks like on a practical level. Flip all the way back to Genesis and let's look into the life of Joseph, a man who displayed forgiveness brilliantly.

First Joseph's back-story: read the following verses. Jot down any pertinent information about Joseph and his relationship with his brothers.

Genesis 37:2-4

Genesis 37:12-36

Joseph's life doesn't get any easier. He was exposed to sexual temptation, punished for doing what was right, imprisoned for years, forgotten by those he helped and betrayed too many times to count. But instead of settling for life as a victim, Joseph remained faithful to God and was elevated both in stature and power.

Now read Genesis 50:15-21. What were Joseph's brothers worried about after their father had died?

Instead what was Joseph's response?

Joseph says, "Am I in the place of God?" (Verse 19). What an amazingly healthy view of himself and the Holy One. Joseph could have used his position to avenge himself but he knew that only God had the authority to judge. Instead, he held fast to the goodness and sovereignty of God.

Write Genesis 50:20 in the space provided.

Now look up Romans 8:28 and write it in the space provided.

Do you notice the similarities? Joseph trusted that in *all things* God works for the good of those who love Him and who have been called according to His purpose. He believed in the redemptive purpose of every circumstance in his life – both good and bad. Instead of placing his disappointments and pain on his brothers, he put them into the hands of his Heavenly Father. There was no grudge held and no bitterness in his heart – only the loving heart of forgiveness.

If forgiveness was possible for Joseph, it's promising for us as well.

Do you take God at His Word when He promises to work everything out for your long term good? If not, what's holding you back from believing?

If there's someone you have yet to forgive, today is the day to place the pains of your past into the nail scared hands of the Savior and walk in the freedom of forgiveness!

Read Ephesians 4:32. What does Paul list as the two prerequisites for forgiveness?

Based on what you've learned about these two characteristics, why do you think they're required when extending forgiveness?

Can I make a little personal note here? It's not by coincidence that as I study and work through each chapter, I've been given the opportunity to practice a little bit of what I'm preaching. After all, if the truth isn't real to me – if I haven't had the opportunity to wrestle with it to some degree –then I certainly have no business talking about it with you.

This morning I encountered an opportunity to forgive, and I didn't want to. When confronted with the choice to forgive (and having just read this verse in Ephesians), I knew what it was going to take to pardon this person. It was going to take some compassion – that deep-seated emotion that profoundly cares – in order to move my heart to care enough to forgive. It was going to take kindness – the covenant love type of kindness – to move me to act beyond how I was feeling. It was also going to have to happen beyond me.

I was going to need a little more practical Biblical advice as to how I was supposed to put on a full measure of forgiveness. You see although I wanted to make the choice to forgive, I was playing the scenes from the morning over and over in my mind. How can I forgive this person if I can't stop the tapes from constantly replaying the event in my head?

Thanks to the ever-inquisitive Peter, we are given more information about how we are to forgive each other.

According to Matthew 18:21-22, how many times does Peter think we should forgive each other?

What is Jesus' response?

Jesus' point about the number isn't that we should keep count of how many times we forgive someone, but that we should forgive them over and over again. When someone offends you, how often do you think about that person and the offense? Each time the offender comes to your mind is an opportunity to forgive. In obedience, we forgive. By faith, we forgive. It's our only worthy response to the forgiveness God graciously bestows on each of us.

Needless to say, today has been a day of practicing forgiveness for me. Every time my mind has tried to race back to the events of the morning, I've chosen to take my critical and accusing thoughts captive and lay them at the feet of Jesus. In my heart I've repeated words of forgiveness and I've prayed over and over for more grace. At the end of the day, I know this to be true: God is honored when I choose to forgive.

The world we live in, unfortunately, operates by a different set of rules. Doesn't it seem like today bitterness is more fashionable than forgiveness? Ladies, this cannot be! Although the world may wear unforgiveness like a merit badge, the same can't be true of a child of the King.

Anger and bitterness may have been part of your everyday wear when dressed in your old wardrobe, but your new style calls for a different set of clothes. Each day as you practice the act of putting on the wardrobe of Jesus Christ, the fabric of forgiveness becomes part of your attire. It's the "bend of Jesus" and therefore who you are in Christ. Step boldly into your new outfit of forgiveness.

DAY 3
LOVE GOD

Can you hear the sound of the proverbial drum roll; we're down to our last article of clothing!

Write Colossians 3:14.

The last piece of clothing: the outer garment of love. With the effect of a binding agent, holding all other virtues in their place, the cloak of love enables all of the other virtues to reach their greatest potential. It's the cornerstone of our faith and the capstone of all other traits.

Read 1 Corinthians 13:1-3.

According to verse 2: Without love, I am _____.

I don't know about you but sometimes I need truth to smack me in the face like a bucket of ice-cold water. This verse does that. The truth is that I'm making noise, wasting time and gaining nothing when I operate outside of love. It makes me wonder: how many hours have I served in vain? How many "heart to heart" conversations have carried no value? The condition of our heart is no secret to God. He always knows our motives, and He commands us to live in love.

There are a few different translations for the word love in the Greek language (like *philos* and *eros*), but the one we are going to focus on from this text is *agape*. *Agape* is not of human affection but a divine love that's produced as fruit in the lives of those fully submitted to Him. Only God is capable of agape love, yet He graciously allows us to experience His unconditional love as Jesus lives through you and me.

I would like to take a quick pause here to reflect for a moment.

If you have your Bible open, please close it. What does your Bible look like? Write a quick description of it. (Is it old or new? What color is it? Is it leather bound? Tabs/No tabs? Big or travel sized? Covered or not? Do you like to write in your bible or keep it clear of ink? What translation is your Bible?)

Each of our Bibles are as different on the outside as the faces that look inside them, but inside will always be the same, regardless of the specific wording or translation. From cover to cover, you Bible is a personal love story: from God to YOU. There's not one dot of ink in the text in your hand that isn't saturated with the love of God. Each story that's told, each command that's given, and each song that's sung – all are written by the God who loves beyond measure and who pursues His beloved beyond all reason.

When was the last time God used His Word to speak straight to your soul as if the words were written for you? Tell us about it.

Take a moment to thank God for His written Word. Thank Him for knowing that we would need something tangible to hold on to - like a love note hidden in our nightstand drawer. With pages tear-stained and words read and re-read until they are etched on your heart – thank God for giving you something that speaks so tenderly to your soul that you have no doubt that this crazy love is true.

Read Matthew 22:36-39. What does Jesus say is the greatest of all commandments?

The most important thing – the tie that holds all else together – is love. We're commanded to love God first. We're told to love God with all that we are: with all our heart, all our soul and all our mind. Have you ever put any thought into what it means to love God in this way?

LOVING GOD WITH ALL YOUR HEART:

Your heart is "the fountain and seat of the thoughts, passions, desires, appetites, affections, purposes, endeavors." According to commentator Albert Barnes, "To love Him with all the heart is to fix the affections supremely on Him, more strongly than on anything else, and to be willing to give up all that we hold dear at His command."[18]

To love God with all of your heart means that He truly is the object of your deepest affection. It means that He's the driving force behind your passions, and He's the one whom you most desire. It means that He's enough. Period. Have I ever really loved God in this way? Have you? Can you really say that you are truly passionate about your relationship with God?

LOVNG GOD WITH ALL YOUR SOUL:

To love God with all of your soul means to love Him with all your "life." Barnes states, "This means, to be willing to give up your life to Him, and to devote it all to His service; to live to Him, and to be willing to die at His command."[19]

Is God really what sustains you? Is He the one that you look to for nourishment of the soul? Do you ever wake up with a desperate need to be filled by your Savior, or is a strong cup of coffee enough to jumpstart your day?

Listen to the words of David in Psalm 63:1.

"O God, you are my God, earnestly I seek you; my soul thirsts for you, my body longs for you, in a dry and weary land where there is no water."

Does your soul ever long for God like that?

LOVING GOD WITH ALL YOUR MIND:

When we love God with all our mind, we choose to submit our "intellect" to His will. Once again according to Barnes, to love Him with all of your mind is "To love His law and gospel more than we do the decisions of our own minds; To be willing to submit all our faculties to His teaching and guidance, and to devote to Him all our intellectual attainments and all the results of our intellectual efforts."[20]

The first question we have to consider here is whether or not we know God's law and His gospel. If His Word is to be our guide in decision making, don't we have to know what it says? When we love God with all of our mind, we are devoted to His written Word and rely on His voice to be our primary navigator in life.

After reading the breakdown of "loving God with our all," what are your initial thoughts about how you are loving God?

All I can say to that is, "Mercy!" That kind of love is profound to me! Before I lose you all together, I want to break up loving God into a few bite-sized pieces we can all digest a little better.

I want to close our day not thinking about how we can love God perfectly (as described previously) but how we can love God more. More is always possible, so that will be our starting place.

Pastor Brian La Croix suggests that by looking at the ways in which we love one another, we can begin to practice some tangible ways to better love our Father in Heaven. In order to do this, we're going to identify with what Dr. Gary Chapman calls the Five Love Languages. After years of counseling, Chapman discovered that most people express and interpret love in five different ways, which he named the Five Love Languages. So, by inspecting each of the love languages, we are going to discover some practical ways in which we can practice loving God more.[21]

#1: WORDS OF AFFIRMATION

How do you usually talk to God? Is most of your communication with God centered on your complaints or everything that's wrong in your world? In order to practice loving God more, consider spending more of your prayer time doting on your Savior. Praise Him for how wonderful He is. Tell him how faithful He has been to you. When we focus on who He is, we can't help but love Him more.

#2: QUALITY TIME

Do you have time set apart in your day for you and God? No distractions - just some good old fashion quality time. God wants nothing more than some alone time with you – to love on you, to speak wisdom to your heart, to comfort you, to teach and encourage you. Do you honor and value Him enough to give Him part of your day? You will be astounded at the way a little one-on-one time can awaken your relationship with the Father.

#3: RECEIVING GIFTS

God bestows upon each one of us a countless number of gifts. Countless. The question is, "Have we received them as gifts from our loving Savior?" Here is my challenge for you: as you go through your day, begin practicing the act of thankfulness. Each time you receive a good and precious gift from God, thank Him for it. It could be the one small act that changes everything.

#4: ACTS OF SERVICE

The best way to serve God is to obey Him.

Read John 14:23-24. How do we show our love of Jesus?

It may be easier to love God emotionally than to love God actively because to actively love Him means to choose obedience regularly. It is this active, obedient love that God is after.

#5: PHYSICAL TOUCH

Are you wondering how we're going to physically touch God? We touch Him by touching the ones He loves. Loving others is a way to show love to God. Tomorrow we will spend our entire study time on loving others so I won't expand on this one today.

Instead, close today thinking practically about how you can love God more.

Which of the love languages could you practice more often in order to actively pursue loving God more?

DAY 4
LOVE OTHERS

We closed yesterday by looking at the five love languages as they each relate to our relationship with God. The final love language, physical touch, is what we're going to focus on today.

How did we say we physically touch God?

Back to Matthew 22:37-39. What does Jesus say is the second greatest command?

In a similar story recorded by Luke, Jesus is questioned further about who qualifies as our neighbor.

Read Luke 10:27-37.

Don't miss the impact of this parable because of familiarity. The story of the Good Samaritan, though often taught in Sunday school, is much more than a lesson for the young. Let's look at the three passersby and consider how we might relate to each.

THE PRIEST: RELIGIOUS AND BUSY

The priest, also known as an expert of the law, came upon the beaten man first, most likely on his way home from Jerusalem where he spent the day praying and worshiping God. At the first glance of the fallen man, the priest quickly crosses to the other side of the road. After all, he can't be bothered by another man's unfortunate circumstance.

This priest might represent those who know the Word backwards and forwards but have never put their knowledge into action. They could be described as, "always learning but never able to acknowledge the truth" (2 Timothy 3:7). They're busy serving God but sadly have little care for the people God came to save. They're diligent to walk the straight and narrow and won't be troubled by people who might make their life messy.

It would be easy for us to point fingers and call out, "Hypocrite!" but let's take a good, long look in the mirror first.

Look up James 1:22-25. How does James describe the person who merely hears the word but doesn't do what it says?

A couple of questions to consider: Are you someone who takes good sermon notes, gets on an emotional high, yells an affirming "Amen", then walks away the same person you were before? Or are you teachable, moldable and pliable in God's hands, able to acknowledge the truth and let it change you forever?

The priest in this story had no time or compassion for the hurting man. Can you relate to him in this way? I think it's fair to say that some are downright slaves to our daily planner. For some of us, each day must be perfectly planned and each minute accounted for with no room for distractions. People like this thrive in the control of their day and if one piece falls out of place, the rest of the day crumbles like a tower of cards.

Are you someone who has your day so perfectly planned and scheduled that you have no time for a phone call from a friend in need or a neighbor with an inconvenient favor? Are you willing to experience life interrupted in order to show somebody the love of God?

Can you think of an opportunity that you might have missed for fear of messing up your schedule or your perfect plans for the day?

THE LEVITE: PLAYS CHURCH BUT NEVER GETS DIRTY

The second man down the road was also a church fellow. The Levite people served as assistants to the priest.

Read 1 Chronicles 23:28-31. List at least 3 duties of the Levites.

Perhaps only a few minutes behind the priest, the Levite was also headed home from a long day at the temple in Jerusalem. Undoubtedly filled with curiosity, he slowed long enough to survey the situation. The New Living translation says, "A Temple assistant walked over and looked at him lying there, but he also passed by on the other side" (Luke 10:32).

The Levite in the story might represent those who have learned to play church well. They attend service regularly and even participate in all of the Bible studies. When the church doors are open, this "Levite" will most likely be there, wearing down the fabric in the exact same seat cushion week after week. They appear to care for the lost and hurting, but their motives are shallow and self-serving. True – they will be the first to share a prayer request for a hurting brother, but they rarely roll up their sleeves and become the answer to the hurting brother's need.

Read 1 John 3:18 and fill in the blanks.

"Dear children, let us not love with _____ or _____ but with _____ and in _____."

Real love isn't a feeling. It's an action. John 3:16 says, "For God so loved the world that he **gave** his one and only Son, that whoever believe in him shall not perish but have eternal life." God didn't give up His only Son because He felt like it. He gave His son because He loved. Love acts. Love sacrifices. Love gives. Our Levite friend might have been the first to tell the story or spread the news, but he missed an opportunity to demonstrate love in action.

Describe a time in your life when you were the recipient of agape love.

THE SAMARITAN: MERCIFUL AND FULL OF LOVE

The last to come upon the fallen man was a Samaritan. The Samaritans were a group of people despised by the Jews. They were considered to be half-breeds, a mixed race of Jewish people from the northern kingdom who intermarried with the gentiles already living in the area. The Samaritan was the least likely to stop and had the least to gain, but to the surprise of all those hearing the tale, he was the one moved by compassion. I don't know if this Samaritan knew the Scriptures, but he lived out the words of Matthew perfectly.

Read Matthew 5:43-47. Who does Jesus say we're to love?

The Samaritans and Jewish people were known to hate each other; they were enemies, but this particular Samaritan man didn't live up to that stereotype. He put love into motion. He showed compassion, gave the man care and paid the cost for him to get back on his feet. He loved as Jesus loved.

So, how do we, like the Good Samaritan, love as Jesus loves us? "By helping when it's not convenient, by giving when it hurts, by devoting energy to other's welfare rather than your own, by absorbing the hurts from others without complaining or fighting back. This kind of loving is difficult to do. That is why people notice when you do it and know that you are empowered by a supernatural source."[22]

Is this type of love really possible? Do we really have it in us to love in such a powerful way? You bet!

Read Romans 5:5. Write it below.

The Spirit of the Living God abides within you. His streams of living water flow within. As long as you surrender your life as an empty vessel waiting to be filled, God's resources will never run dry. The strength isn't in how much love your heart can hold, but how much God will pour in and through you. Measure God's ability to love, not your own. He will never disappoint.

Read the following verses. Note how each encourages you in the strength of God's love.

Romans 8:38-39

1 Corinthians 13:4-8

Ephesians 3:17-19

1 John 4:7-21

Do you know and trust in the love of God? Have you experienced it personally? If so, today's the day to begin to rely on His love as you reach out to others. Step out in faith. One arm at a time lets sink into the cloak of love – and watch as God's love is made complete. It's an opportunity with eternal possibilities each and every day.

DAY 5
A REFRESHER COURSE

I start today with an important question: Can you handle some brutal honesty before we bring this study to a close?

OK. Here it is … I have no idea how to bring this study to a close! Really. None.

I've sat and stared at the blinking cursor of my computer screen for longer than I care to admit. I've checked my email, read and reread all of my favorite home decorating blogs and walked away to do whatever else imaginable to distract me from the task at hand. It's been days, weeks….OK, it's been months.

It's no secret: I'm not a great finisher. There are incomplete projects all around my house that bare testimony to my lack of finish-ability. But this study – ladies, we're going to find a way to finish!

Maybe the best way to end is to go back to the start. Every time I complete a Bible study or even a great book, I go back through and re-read the things I underlined, starred or highlighted. I refuse to make it to the end unchanged. So, I re-visit the moments when my eyes were opened. I refresh my mind with the things that caused a stir in me, the truths that made me squirm in conviction, or the words that inspired me to change. After all, that's how we participate in the transformation process of becoming more like Jesus.

I'd like to spend the day reminiscing, reviewing and summing up our study of The Wardrobe of Christ.

Let's start with our memory verse. Before I challenge you to write Colossians 3:12-14 out by memory, I would like you to read it again from The Message.

"So, chosen by God for this new life of love, dress in the wardrobe God picked out for you: compassion, kindness, humility, quiet strength, discipline. Be even-tempered, content with second place, quick to forgive an offense. Forgive as quickly and completely as the Master forgave you. And regardless of what else you put on, wear love. It's your basic, all-purpose garment. Never be without it."

So good, isn't it? "Dress in the wardrobe God picked out for you" … yes! For over a year now that concept has been spinning around in my mind like clothes in a dryer set on permanent press with no off switch. As I get dressed each day I think of it … God has a wardrobe picked out for me. Will I put it on today? The answer seems simple. Yes! Of course I want to wear this heavenly attire. But after completing this study, I know my answer always comes with a choice. And a death.

If I'm going to choose His way, I have to die to mine. If I'm going to participate today in the great exchange, I have to be willing to surrender. I must deny the old self and the baggage packed heavy in the backpack that it carries. Am I truly offended by my old self … that old part of me that thrives on independence and feelings and approval? Or is that comfort wear to me?

By now I know what the new self has to offer and I know I want to put it on. It offers a brand new identity, a new way of thinking and an upside-down way of living. It asks me to keep my eyes fixed on things above, to settle into my hiding place and shine with the light of Jesus for the whole world to see.

Oh … and it offers the most glorious wardrobe!

But wait. Before I go on in my reminiscing, you have a verse to write. (You thought I forgot, didn't you?) Please try to write Colossians 3:12-14 by memory. You can peek if you need to or use the verse out of The Message as a cheat sheet.

As I write out these verses again, I can't help but smile on the inside as I read, "chosen, holy and dearly loved". The truth that I'm one of God's favorites will not be wasted on me. Some days it's the thing that enables me to lift my head up off of my fluffy white pillow and greet the day. It's what motivates me to live beyond the all-consuming "me, myself and I." It's what gives me the courage to hit the keys as I type. Knowing who – no, whose – I am is everything to me.

How have you grown in your understanding of your identity in Christ while doing this study?

With our identity now settled, we are then presented with this miraculous wardrobe – a supernatural set of clothes - and we're told to put them on….

Can you remember all of the virtues that we're commanded to put on, according to Colossians 3:12-14? List each character trait and write a definition for each based on what you have learned.

I wake up each morning determined to get it right, filled with nothing but good intentions. I rehearse the list again in my head: compassion, kindness, humility, gentleness, patience, forgiveness and love. Got it. I can do this. But how is it only noon and I've lost it already? As good as my good intentions are, they are not good enough.

Putting on this wardrobe involves more than just good behavior. How did I forget already: the wardrobe of Christ always demands a choice and a death. In this process of learning how to dress well, I have so much I have to unlearn first. My mind needs more truth: "He must become greater; I must become less." (John 3:30)

Slowly – daily – transformation is happening. Every time I walk towards those in pain instead of running happily along my merry way, transformation is happening. Every time I serve when it's inconvenient or put another before myself, transformation is happening. Every time I live in the moment and show mercy to the incompetent, transformation is happening. Each time I choose to forgive and show love to the unlovely, transformation is happening.

Each time I yield to Christ in me, the transformation is really happening.

Now it's your turn. As you look back through the weeks that we have spent together, was there something God spoke to you about – something personal that will assist you as you get dressed each day? Was there something you learned in the last six weeks that you're certain God wants to use in your transformation process? (Of course you are not limited to one but if one truth is all you can tuck into your purse on your way out the door, then one thing is enough!)

The wardrobe of Christ: it's only through Jesus, my friends. Will you choose to put it on today?

LEADER GUIDE

Introduction: For the leader

This leader guide will help you set up and lead your group. As the leader, your responsibility is to review each weekly lesson by asking questions and facilitating discussion.

Participating in a Bible study with other ladies is one of my favorite things to do and one of the most important parts of my life. Whether we say it out loud or not, we're all seeking community. There's no better place than a Bible study to create lasting community among friends. As you go through this study, use the time you have together to invest in building relationships. No matter how well acquainted you are with the members of your group before the study begins, be intentional about pursuing each of them for the next ten weeks. Commit to praying for your group members, and let them know each week that you're thinking of them.

Participating with a small group Bible study also keeps us accountable to spending intentional time in the Word. With so many different things vying for our time and attention, sometimes it takes the accountability of a group to get us to pick up our Bibles. I understand. I've been there. Challenge your group members to put in the work for the next ten weeks in order to complete each lesson. This may mean that some may need to fast from something in their normal routine in order to make time for Bible study. Do it! You will be blessed more than you know! {Fasting? That means that you give up something for a time in order to focus your attention on the Lord. What's competing most for your time? TV shows, Facebook, Pinterest, another hobby? Are you willing to give that up for a time in order to make time for the Word?}

Before you begin, here are a couple quick tips for leading a small group.

* Pray. Pray when you're together. Pray when you're apart. Pray for each other. God is listening!
* Read through the questions before you meet with your group so that you know in advance what you'll be discussing together.
* Comfort is key. It's important that every member of the group feels comfortable sharing during discussion time. Try to keep one person from dominating discussions by gently moving the conversation to others in the group. If there's someone who would rather not talk, that's ok too.
* You might need to be brave first. Relationships and accountability grow out of honest, open discussions. You may have to be the first one to dig deep to tell a personal story but I promise you won't be the last.

Chapter 1: Clothed in Christ

1. Spend the first few minutes getting to know the members in your group. Have everyone introduce themselves by saying their name and answering an ice-breaker question. It could be a funny quirk they have, what they slept in the night before, the grossest thing they've ever eaten- anything that will loosen everyone up and get them talking.
2. Is Jesus 'comfort wear' to you? Discuss why or why not.
3. From Day 1: "…when Jesus bids us to come, He is actually inviting us to come and stay." Does the call to *abide* challenge you in any way? Practically speaking, how can you make Jesus a part of your everyday wear?
4. Which of the three names of the Son of God resonate most with you? Why?
5. Give an example of how the flesh rebels against the law of Truth?
6. From Day 4: "If we don't control our thought life, Satan will use our thoughts to control us." Although we'll spend more time talking about this in the weeks ahead, spend some time talking about the battle going on in our thought life. Do you typically allow your feelings to be your guide? How's that working out for you?
7. How do you relate to the examples given at the end of Day 4?
8. Discuss the struggles you have regarding independent living.
9. How have you bought into the lie that you have to work hard and be good in order to win God's approval?
10. Ask someone to read Galatians 5:1. In light of what you learned this week, discuss what this freedom could and should look like. Spend your last few minutes in prayer, thanking God for the freedom we have in Christ Jesus!

Chapter 2: The New You

The material in this chapter is foundational. There may be members in your group who have never participated in the Great Exchange that is discussed in Day 2. Be sensitive to group members who may have more questions about what it means to accept Jesus as their personal Savior. Make time to walk them through the process of salvation, and if they are ready, pray with them to receive Jesus as their Lord and Savior.

1. Open in prayer.
2. "If you agree to fully step into your new self, the entire old self has to go. Remember, the old self has no redeeming qualities." Throughout the week, has God brought to mind any parts of the old self that you have not yet thrown away?
3. After filling in the chart in Day 2, discuss the profound effect of the Great Exchange. Practically speaking, talk about what it means to exchange your life for His.
4. Put into your own words what it means to be transformed.
5. Take turns reading a couple of the verses listed at the start of Day 3. How do these verses reveal the importance of knowing and meditating on the Word of God?
6. Spend some time going over the "long list of whatever's" in Day 3. Can you think of practical ways you can apply this list as you evaluate what thoughts are acceptable in the mind of a Child of the King?

7. Discuss Posture #1: The new self sets its gaze upwards. How do you use your time to reflect your first priority? How could you make better use of your time to seek God as your first priority?

8. Discuss Posture #2: The new self learns to settle into its hiding place. Share a specific time when Jesus made Himself known to you as a refuge.

9. Discuss some of the ways that you personally hide the light of Jesus by living like a "bucket-head".

10. Close your time together by praying that each of you would allow the radiant light of Jesus to shine through you in unique and powerful ways this week.

Chapter 3: Compassion and Kindness

1. Open in a word of prayer.

2. Did everyone write Colossians 3:12-14 on a note card to memorize? Discuss the different ways you practice memorizing verses. Can anyone share a great tip that's helped you to put God's Word to memory?

3. Spend a few minutes talking about what you learned as you read through the three descriptive words used to describe all Christ followers: "Chosen, holy, dearly loved."

4. Which of these three identity words do you struggle with most? Why?

5. Describe a time in your life when God revealed His tender compassions to you.

6. What or who do you usually turn to when you need comfort? Why? How can you begin to practice turning to God for comfort instead of those other comfort substitutes?

7. In Day 3, we discussed three ways that God comforts His children. Which way do you most often experience the comfort of God?

8. What do the words "Me too" mean to you when you are going through a struggle? Discuss different ways that God can use you to be someone else's "Me too".

9. Jesus showed kindness along His way. It was His intentional response to the compassion He felt as He came across those in need. Discuss the ways you are challenged to show kindness to your family and beyond.

10. Close your discussion time in prayer.

Chapter 4: Humility

1. Open in prayer.

2. How's the memorization going? Has everyone been practicing their verses? Can anyone recite Colossians 3:12-14 by memory yet? How about just verse 12?

3. Someone read Philippians 2:3-4. Can you think of three practical ways you can 'consider others better than yourself'?

4. Discuss how the sacrifice of praise is supposed to be a fruit of your lips, not a work (page 59). Share with the group a specific time that you offered a sacrifice of praise and how God used it during that dark season?

5. What does it mean to present your vessel to God?

6. "Our submission is manifested in ready obedience to the Lord." How are you doing in the area of obedience? Is there some part of your life where you're having a difficult time 'just obeying'?

7. Serving always begins at home. Read Colossians 3:23-24. How does Jesus' attitude in serving challenge you when serving your family? What about those outside your home?

8. Share with the group some of the action statements you listed at the end of Day 4.

9. "Humility is a choice. It's a deliberate act." When is it most difficult for you to humble yourself?

10. Spend your last few minutes praying together.

Chapter 5: Gentleness and Patience

1. Open in prayer. Practice saying your memory verses out loud together.

2. Based on what you read in Day 1, did you need to change your perception of gentleness? Discuss how/why with the group.

3. Read through the four strengths of the meek in Day 1. Which characteristic challenges you the most?

4. Ask someone to read Isaiah 30:15. Discuss what it means to have a "quiet" spirit. Is that your reality? If not, what's it going to take for you to get there?

5. Do you struggle with any of the listed characteristics of those that are teachable? (Quick to listen, slow to speak, slow to become angry) Discuss how you think you are doing in the area of being teachable.

6. Without naming names, discuss the ways that God may be using those "holy sandpaper" people to bring about change in you.

7. Can you describe a time in your life when God answered your cry to Him by giving you the indescribable gift of peace instead of the answer you thought you were longing for?

8. Are you in a season of wait? Does the meaning of the word wait ("to bind together by twisting") change your perception of waiting? If so, how?

9. Can you give evidence from your own life that attests to the fact that Jesus' power is made perfect in our weaknesses?

10. Close in a time of prayer.

Chapter 6: Forgiveness and Love

1. Open in prayer. Did everyone memorize their verses? Let those who can quote the verse from memory for the rest of the group.

2. After going through the checklist in the introduction to week six, do you still struggle with feeling like you have to work hard to put on these virtues? Discuss with your group your struggle, if any, of still trying to perform for God instead of simply deferring to Him to live out these virtues through you.

3. Ask a few group members to read the verse they labeled with a star on Day 1 and explain why/how it spoke to them. Do you struggle with receiving the forgiveness of God?

4. Read Ephesians 4:32 together. Based on what you've learned about these two characteristics, why do you think they're required when extending forgiveness?

5. Discuss the "seventy-seven times" principle of forgiveness and how it actually plays out in your life.

6. Discuss what it means to love God with all your heart, soul and mind. What are your initial thoughts about how you are loving God?

7. Which of the love languages could you practice more often in order to actively pursue loving God more?

8. In the familiar story about the Good Samaritan, which of the passersby do you relate to most? Why?

9. What's your biggest take home from this study?

10. Pray together as you close, thanking God for all He's done and will continue to do in each of our lives.

ACKNOWLEDGEMENTS

Erik: You read as I went, encouraged and never let me quit – even when I thought it stunk – thank you. I love you!

Haley, Rylie and Coleman: You give me so many opportunities to practice what I preach and I love you for it! Thank you for allowing me to "do bible study".

Mom, Dad and Mindy: Thank you for a lifetime of love and support.

Mary Kay: My mentor and friend. Thank you for asking questions, listening, challenging and loving me. What would I do without you?

Pastor Randy: Thank you for seeing more in me than I see in myself and for challenging me to dream.

Amanda: Your friendship has been a source of strength for me now for 20 years. Thank you for digging in with me, for doing research and rough drafts edits. This is yours too!

Jody, Larissa, Libby, Brittney, Shannon and Jen W.: You are God's gift to me! Thanks for being the first to do the study, for helping make it better, for giving it a title – and most of all for being my best friends. I love y'all!

Christy and Jen G.: I love doing life with you! Thanks for cheering me on in all my "projects"!

NOTES

1   *Exhaustive Concordance of the Bible.* Anaheim, CA: Foundation Publications, INC., 1998, 1546.

2   Murray, Andrew. *Abide in Christ.* New Kensington, PA: Whitaker House, 1979.

3   Zodhiates, Spiros Th.D. *The Complete Word Study Dictionary.* Chattanooga, TN: AMG Publishers, 1992.

4   Miller, J.R. *The Hidden Life.* New York: Thomas Y. Crowell & Company, 1895.

5   *Life Application Study Bible, New International Version.* Grand Rapids, Michigan: Tyndale House Publishers, Inc., 2005.

6   Bell, Rob. *Jesus Wants to Save Christians.* Grand Rapids, MI : Zondervan, 2008.

7   Murray, Andrew. *Humility.* New Kensington, PA: Whitaker House, 1982.

8   Dieleman, Adrian Rev. "Honor One Another." 10 Oct. 1999

9   *Life Application Study Bible, New International Version.* Grand Rapids, Michigan: Tyndale House Publishers, Inc., 2005.

10 Piper, John. "Blessed Are The Meek." 9 Feb 1986.

11 Voskamp, Ann. *One Thousand Gifts.* Grand Rapids, MI: Zondervan, 2010.

12 Piper, John. "The Sacrifice of Praise". http://www.desiringgod.org/resource-library/sermons/the-sacrifice-of-praise

13 Tozer, A.W. http://www.preceptaustin.org/romans_12_word_studies.htm

14 Spurgeon, C.H. "Unconditional Surrender." At the Metropolitan Tabernacle, Newington, 30 Jan 1876

15 Henry, Matthew. *Commentary On The Whole Bible.* Grand Rapids, MI: Zondervan Publishing House, 1961.

16 Bill, Bryan. "The Gentleness of Jesus." http://www.moody.edu/edu_AlumniGenDetail.aspx?id=38118

17 Ibid.

18 Barnes, Albert. http://www.ccel.org/ccel/barnes/ntnotes.iv.xxii.xxxvii.html

19 Ibid.

20 Ibid.

21 La Croix, Brian. "Loving God with All Your Heart and Soul." http://www.sermoncentral.com/sermons/loving-god-with-all-your-heart-and-soul-brian-la-croix-sermon-on-love-for-god-142909.asp?page=2

22 *Life Application Study Bible, New International Version.* Grand Rapids, Michigan: Tyndale House Publishers, Inc., 2005.